Lonny
Willis
HC

BLOODY AACHEN

By the same author

FINALE AT FLENSBURG
HUNTERS FROM THE SKY
THE BATTLE FOR TWELVELAND
WEREWOLF

CHARLES WHITING

BLOODY AACHEN

STEIN AND DAY/*Publishers*/New York

First published in the United States of America, 1976
Copyright © 1976 by Charles Whiting
All rights reserved
Printed in the United States of America
Stein and Day/*Publishers*/Scarborough House,
Briarcliff Manor, N.Y. 10510

Library of Congress Cataloging in Publication Data
Whiting, Charles, 1926–
  Bloody Aachen.

  1. Aachen—Siege, 1944. I. Title.
D757.9.A2W48   940.54′21   76-10132
ISBN 0-8128-2090-3

AUTHOR'S ACKNOWLEDGMENT

THIS book would not have been possible without the dedicated aid of one man, Herr Wolfgang Trees of Aachen.

Chief-reporter in his native Aachen, DJ on Belgian Radio, amateur farmer in the Dutch village where he lives, local historian of the three-country border area, German TV commentator (the list of his activities seems endless), he is a typical example of the new 'European' who has forgotten national differences. With his typical energy and enthusiasm, he threw himself into the task of finding the survivors of that terrible battle which took place in the city of his birth when he was barely one year old. Thanks to Wolfgang Trees I obtained all the information I needed. It was also Herr Trees who carried out all the interviews with the German and Dutch participants of the Battle. I owe him a very special debt of gratitude.

I must also express my deepest thanks to Dr Konrad Simon, the Editor-in-Chief of Aachen's major newspaper, another dedicated European, who was kind enough to put the full resources of the unique *Aachener Volkszeitung*, with its daily German, Belgian and Dutch editions (surely the only daily of its kind in Europe) at my disposal.

And finally a last word of thanks to the people, who lived through *Bloody Aachen* and who responded so wholeheartedly to my requests for information. It is to them—and the white-haired, elderly American gentlemen, who once fought against them as hard, vital young men—that this book is dedicated. *To the survivors!*

C.W.

ILLUSTRATIONS

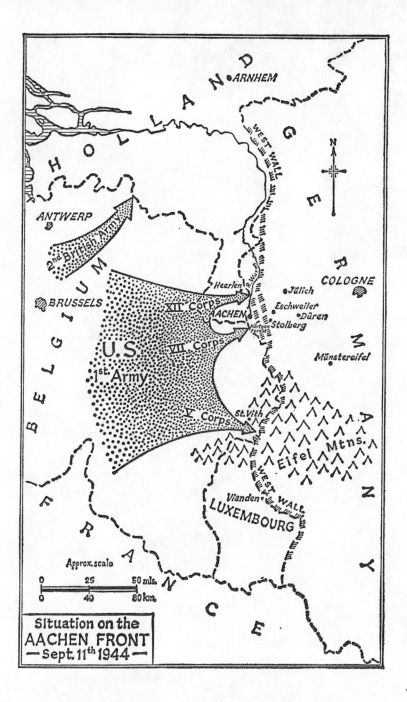

Situation on the
AACHEN FRONT
— Sept. 11th 1944 —

BLOODY AACHEN

INTRODUCTION

On the morning of Thursday, 16 September, 1944, Adolf Hitler concluded his daily conference at his East Prussian HQ, 'Wolf's Lair', by inviting his most trusted military advisers to meet him later for a second conference.

Half an hour later they began to assemble in the sparsely furnished, wooden operations room, the soldiers and airmen who had run the *Wehrmacht* for the last five years: Field Marshal Keitel, wooden and stiff; Colonel-General Jodl, pale-faced and cunning; Colonel-General Heinz Guderian, the tank expert; General Kreipe, the *Luftwaffe's* elegant representative. But, in spite of the enormous power at their command, these high-ranking officers whispered to one another while they waited like schoolboys for the appearance of the headmaster.

Finally Hitler appeared. He did not make a good impression. His gait was slow. His blue eyes were faded and distant. He did not look like the man who had commanded Germany's destiny for the last twelve years and had made her—for a time at least—the ruler of the whole of Europe from the Urals to the English Channel. Untidily Hitler slumped down on the hard wooden chair at the head of the table and nodded to Jodl, his Chief-of-Staff, to begin this unexpected conference.

Jodl, perhaps the only one of the *Wehrmacht's* high-ranking commanders to enjoy his confidence after the generals' plot on Hitler's life the previous July, launched into a swift, objective account of Germany's situation in this fifth year of the war. Now the Reich was without Allies. One by one they had changed sides during the previous months or begun peace negotiations. Even the 'honorary Aryans' in the East, Germany's Japanese Allies, had politely suggested that the Reich should sue for peace with the Russians. Colonel Jodl swiftly sketched in Germany's military losses in both East and West, remarking that since July, 1944, the *Wehrmacht* had suffered over a million casualties, most of them incurred in France and Belgium since the Western Allies had broken out of the Normandy bridgeheads. In essence, eight whole German combat divisions had been wiped out in the West since 1 August!

Jodl let them absorb the information for a moment before going on to assure them that there was, nevertheless, a faint glimmer of hope on the horizon. The Russian summer offensive through Eastern Poland seemed to have run out of steam, whereas the Western Allies' offensive was beginning to slow down. 'On the Western Front,' he said, 'we're getting a real rest in the Ardennes.'

The word 'Ardennes' jerked Hitler out of his reverie. 'Stop!' he cried and raised his hand dramatically.

Jodl stopped.

'I have made a momentous decision. I am taking the offensive. Here—out of the Ardennes!' Hitler smashed his fist down on an unrolled general staff map in front of him on the table. 'Across the Meuse and on to Antwerp!'

The generals stared at him. The old man who had entered the conference room minutes before was transformed. His blue eyes blazed with their old fervour. The man facing them now was the Hitler of that great year of victories— 1940. They felt the first faint stirrings of new hope.

Thus on that September morning in the East Prussian forest of Rastenburg, which housed Hitler's HQ, the last great German offensive in the West was born. Three months later, in the snowy forests of the Ardennes, it materialized as the US Army's major battle of the whole war in Europe—the Battle of the Bulge.

But that September, Hitler's Germany faced imminent collapse. The enemy was at the gates in seemingly overwhelming strength. Even a suddenly enthusiastic, revitalized Führer knew he needed time in order to organize, arm and train the estimated twelve tank and eighteen infantry divisions—a quarter of a million men or more—he wanted for the great new offensive, which would split the Western Allies and force them to offer Germany a more favourable peace. *Time!* But where would he find it? Would the Allies allow him the respite he so desperately needed?

Unknown to Hitler that day, a small American armoured force, commanded by the son of an Eastern European rabbi, was already engaged in an operation which would eventually give him all the time he needed. On that Saturday, the tanks of General Maurice Rose's 3rd Armored Division, the 'Spearhead', were pushing against the outer defences of the great frontier city of Aachen.

Rose's Corps Commander, the dynamic 'Lightning Joe' Collins, called the operation 'a reconnaissance in force' and maintained that the old Imperial German city would be taken 'on the bounce'; then his VII Corps could drive hell-for-leather for the last natural barrier in Germany, the River Rhine.

In fact, the battle for the first German city to bar the Allied advance into the Reich lasted six weeks and cost the

American First Army an estimated eight thousand men, killed, wounded and missing, not to mention two hundred tanks. When the battle to force Aachen's flank in the Hurtgen Forest was over, the US First Army had been fought to a standstill. When it resumed operations, its lead divisions ran straight into the initial assault in the Ardennes. After Aachen, it was another four months before the Allies really started to move into Germany again; although in that September Field-Marshal Montgomery confidently predicted that Germany would surrender by Christmas. Indeed he even wagered a fiver with General Eisenhower on that 'certainty'.

But the tired infantrymen of the 'Big Red One', the American army's premier division, who fought the Battle of Aachen, knew differently. Told by Ed Wilcox, correspondent of the *Warweek* magazine, that he would be home by Christmas, 1944, one rifleman grinned wearily and said: 'Sure if the fighting to come is like this in Aachen, I'll be home for Christmas all right—*Christmas in two years' time!*'

For the US Army, the Battle of Aachen was a unique fight. For the first time in its 168-year history it besieged a German city.* But that wasn't all. For this was a city with a difference. Aachen was an imperial city, where 32 German Emperors and Kings had been crowned over 1,000 years, a symbol of German nationalism, part of the National Socialist mythology. It was also Germany's premier Catholic city, many of whose citizens actively opposed the 'godless' Nazi régime. Indeed 20,000 of them, including Aachen's Bishop, went 'underground', when the Nazis ordered the city's evac-

* There were two similar sieges of German cities—the three-month Russian siege of Breslau and the two-week British siege of Bremen in April, 1945.

uation at the commencement of the battle; and when the Americans finally triumphed, they were welcomed almost as liberators and asked why they had taken so long to defeat the *Wehrmacht* defenders and 'free us'.

Thus, more than thirty years ago, a strange, three-sided battle began in Charlemagne's ancient city. The two opposing armies met in open combat, with the Germans fighting desperately to gain time for their Führer to launch his decisive offensive. But underground in the shattered ruins and cellars, a third force tried to survive, Aachen's men, women and children, persecuted by both sides. By the Nazis because they had refused to be evacuated at the Führer's express command; by the Americans because they were the 'enemy'.

In the end the Americans triumphed. After six long, hard-slogging weeks when progress was often measured in yards, they conquered the old imperial city. But it was a pyrrhic victory. The US First Army had been fought to a standstill; and exactly two months later, on 16 December, 1944, German infantry started to stream out of the fir forests of the Eifel less than twenty miles away from Aachen to begin the Battle of the Bulge, which was to cost the Americans 80,000 casualties and delay the end of the Second World War by another six months.

This, then, is the story of a unique battle, recorded in book-form for the very first time, the story of BLOODY AACHEN.

BOOK ONE:
A RECONNAISSANCE IN FORCE

'Suddenly there was Germany spread out before us!'
Ernest Hemingway, Tuesday, 12 September,
1944

CHAPTER ONE

THE young American Sergeant stared at the wrecked bridge. Only hours before the retreating Germans had destroyed it. Now its ruins lay in the River Our, blocking the way ahead for the point of the US 5th Armored Division. 'What are we going to do, Sarge?' Corporal Ralph Driver asked him. 'That water sure looks deep.'

The Sergeant, in charge of the five-man patrol, did not answer. The shadows were already beginning to lengthen and he knew he did not have much time left before dark. All the same the Divisional Commander, back at his CP on the Luxembourg side of the border, was screaming out for information. It was now or never. He had to make a decision—and soon.

'Okay, men,' he called to the others, crouched in the undergrowth which lined the bank of the river, their weapons at the alert. 'We're going across.' He nodded to Delille, their French guide who had been with the Maquis, 'You follow after me.'

Raising his carbine to his chest, the Sergeant stepped into the fast-running river. The water reached to his knees, then his thighs. Now he had reached the half-way mark. The opposite bank was still silent. Strung out behind him, Delille, Corporal Driver, Privates Locke and McNeath were also past the half-way mark. With a grunt, the Sergeant tugged himself out and stepped on to the muddy bank of the enemy side. There was no sound save for the steady rumble of the heavy guns in the distance; no reaction from the Germans, who could well be hidden on the heights above.

'Okay, men,' he ordered. 'Spread out! We're going to check out those buildings up there—and then we're gonna get the hell out of here *quick!*' Like the experienced soldiers they were, the men advanced cautiously up the slope towards the heights, upon which perched what appeared to be a cluster of poor, run-down farmhouses.

But they weren't. When they reached them, the buildings, which obviously had been hastily abandoned a few hours before, proved to be the cunningly camouflaged bunkers of what the Germans called the West Wall. It was the 'Siegfried Line' on which the British Tommies had boasted in 1939 that they would hang out their 'washing'.

The patrol made a hurried inspection of the twenty concrete bunkers, around one of which someone had built a very un-military chicken coop. Then they had seen enough. The sun had almost vanished beyond the heights and the night was already beginning to poke long black fingers into the valley below. It was time to return the way they had come and report their news to their superiors. 'Let's get the hell out of here!' the Sergeant snapped.

His men needed no urging. They didn't want to be caught out here in the open. As soon as it grew dark and they were free from the danger of attack by the feared *Jabos*, low-flying Allied fighter-bombers, the Germans would surely come flooding back. Ten minutes later they had re-crossed the River Our and were doubling towards their parked White half-track. Thirty minutes after that they were reporting their discovery to the 85th Reconnaissance Squadron's intelligence officer. Sixty minutes later the news was on its way to no less a person than General Courtney Hodges, the commander of the half-a-million strong US First Army, to which the 5th Armored Division belonged. The brief report, couched in the dry unemotional prose of the time, read:

'At 1805 hours on 11 September, a patrol led by S. Sgt Warner W. Holzinger crossed into Germany near the village of Stolzemburg, a few miles north-east of Vianden, Luxembourg.'

For the first time since the days of Napoleon, an enemy soldier had set foot on German territory during wartime. Staff-Sergeant Holzinger had returned to the land of his forefathers.

Soon other American patrols began to cross the frontier into the Reich, from Luxembourg and Belgium on a front of sixty or more miles between Vianden and Raeren. All that warm September night, patrol after patrol crept cautiously into Nazi Germany. Thus by the morning of Tuesday, 12 September, 1944, the khaki-clad tide was washing against and over the length of the frontier in the Eifel–Ardennes area and recce patrols everywhere were reporting excitedly to their superior officers that 'the Krauts have just gone and vanished!'

Ernest Hemingway, then enjoying himself hugely as a war correspondent attached to the US 4th 'Ivy League' Infantry Division, was with one such patrol of the Fourth's 22nd Infantry. Many years later he recalled watching a German half-track 'scuttle like an animal out of a forest', as the patrol advanced towards Hemmeres, south-east of the Belgian border town of St Vith. But the lone half-track did not stop the patrol's progress and then 'suddenly,' as Hemingway wrote, 'there was Germany spread out before us!'

Pausing behind a big haystack, Hemingway stopped to watch as the 4th's artillery blasted a path free for the infantry and then the GIs crossed a ford—'water brown over brown mossy stones'—and stopped once again to watch the first American tanks enter Germany. It was now four-thirty in the afternoon.

A few minutes later Hemingway passed through Hemmeres, its cobbled, debris-littered streets lined with 'ugly women and squat, ill-shaped men' who came towards him with bottles of schnapps, drinking some themselves to show that they were not poisoned. All the houses were deserted, Hemingway noted, but in one he found the still warm remains of a German officer's dinner.

The sight of food made Hemingway think of his own stomach. In his usual arrogant manner, he requisitioned a farmhouse, shot the heads off some chickens with his forty-five and ordered a frightened middle-aged woman to cook them. Then he invited his old buddy, Colonel Lanham, commander of the 22nd Infantry, and his staff to dinner.

That evening the writer and his guests ate on German soil for the first time, and Lanham, an amateur writer and professional soldier who would soon lose a third of his regiment less than thirty miles from where he was now enjoying himself, thought that the farmhouse dinner was 'his happiest night of the whole war'. As he wrote later:

'The food was excellent, the wine plentiful, the comradeship close and warm. All of us were heady with the taste of victory, as we were with the wine. It was a night to put aside the thought of the great West Wall against which we would throw ourselves in the next forty-eight hours. We laughed and drank and told horrendous stories about each other. We all seemed for the moment like minor gods and Hemingway presiding at the head of the table might have been a fatherly Mars delighting in the happiness of his brood.'

Far to the rear the Supreme Commander, General Dwight D. Eisenhower, had already decided what would happen to those happy young men.

On Wednesday, 5 September, 1944, General Eisenhower was confined to his HQ 'Shellburst'* at Granville on the Normandy coast. He had injured his 'good' knee—his 'bad' knee had been permanently damaged at West Point thirty years earlier—during an emergency landing on the beach. Now, with it strapped in a rubber bandage and resting on a stool in front of him, Eisenhower considered his position. It seemed to him to be excellent. Since the August breakout from the beach-heads, his armies had advanced from Falaise to Antwerp, to Namur and on to Verdun, destroying eight German divisions and liberating Paris and Brussels in the process. Everywhere the Germans were crumbling and running for their lives.

But what would they do once they came back to their own frontier? As he had told his General Marshall, who had made Eisenhower Supreme Commander over the heads of 300-odd other general officers, the day before: 'The closer we get to the Siegfried Line, the more we will be stretched administratively and eventually a period of relative inaction will be imposed upon us.' The danger then might be that 'while we are temporarily stalled the enemy will be able to pick up the bits and pieces of forces everywhere and reor-

* A singularly inapt name when one considers Granville was some 300 miles behind the front, with hardly a great possibility of many shells bursting there.

ganize them swiftly for defending the Siegfried Line or the Rhine.'

His own recipe was to keep the Germans 'stretched everywhere', so that they wouldn't have a chance to build up a firm defensive line. In other words, once his armies came to the West Wall, he would not halt them. They would attack and break through it without pause. But where?

On that September day, Eisenhower made his decision and dictated it as a memorandum to his secretary: 'For some days it has been obvious that our military forces can advance almost at will, subject only to the requirements for maintenance. Resistance has largely melted all along the front. From the beginning of this campaign, I have always envisaged that as soon as substantial destruction of the enemy forces in France could be accomplished, we should advance rapidly on the Rhine by pushing through the Aachen Gap in the north and through the Metz Gap in the south. The virtue of this movement is that it takes advantage of all existing lines of communication in the advance towards Germany and brings the southern forces on the Rhine at Coblenz, practically on the flank of the forces that would advance straight through Aachen. I see no reason to change this conception.'

That day the die was cast. The attack on Aachen was on. For the first time in over a century, an attack was going to be launched on a German city by land.

CHAPTER TWO

'AQUAE GRANI' the Romans had called the remote German settlement where thirty springs flowed from a depth of 8,000 feet at temperatures of up to 75° centigrade; and to which they had sent their sick soldiers to be cured in the springs' healing waters.

The French had combined the concept of springs (*Aix*) and the palace chapel (*Chapelle*), built by Charlemagne himself, also attracted there by the warm medicinal springs, and entitled it 'Aix-la-Chapelle'. In their turn, the Czechs had named it 'Cachy', the Poles 'Akwizgranie' and the Italians 'Aquisgran'. But its original pagan Germanic inhabitants had called it after the Old German word for water 'Ahha', which, in due course, became the city's present name —Aachen.

Water had made Aachen. From the times of the Romans, through those of Charlemagne, who was buried there, to those of the thirty-two medieval German kings and emperors who were crowned in the city, its healing springs had attracted pilgrims and the sick from all over Europe. They had made Aachen wealthy and powerful, and rich in cultural treasures so that when its healing waters were no longer sought after, others followed to admire the city itself. Peter the Great of Russia, Handel, Frederick the Great, Clive of India, Bismarck, Roosevelt—had all come to admire the splendid memorials to the past.

But by September, 1944, there was little left to admire in

the old Imperial City. In the seventy-five large scale air-raids the city had suffered since the outbreak of war, 43% of its buildings had been destroyed and another 40% badly damaged. Twenty-five churches had gone and 50% of the schools. An estimated 3 million square metres of debris covered the once famed inner city. Of the 162,000 citizens who had lived there in 1939, by then only 25,000 eked out a miserable existence in cellars and bunkers. That September men no longer came to Aachen to admire; they came to kill and be killed!

The job of taking this vast ruin was given to General Hodges, commander of the US First Army. But the General was not so confident about the possible success of his mission as was Eisenhower, far away in Granville. Although the Army Group Commander, General Bradley, described him as 'one of the most skilled craftsmen' under his command, Hodges was by nature cautious and perhaps too careful, not given to taking risks. In the opinion of one of his tank commanders, General Harmon of the 2nd Armored, a general in the Patton tradition, 'the First Army remained to me a typical infantryman's operations—slow, cautious and without too much zip'.

But the West Wall fortifications around Aachen were indeed formidable. They consisted of deep belts of elaborately inter-connected pillboxes and bunkers, some of them with walls two yards thick. And in places the fortified lines, built in the mid-thirties, reached to a depth of ten miles. An attack on Aachen, however weak its defenders, would be no walkover.

Besides, as Hodges told his three corps commanders, Generals Corlett, Gerow and Collins on the day he received Eisenhower's order to attack his supplies were running out.

Wouldn't it be best if First Army halted for a couple of days and waited for fresh supplies of petrol and ammunition? Hodges' closest adviser thought otherwise. General Joe Collins, a dynamic 48-year-old had gained the nickname of 'Lightning Joe' by his flamboyant handling of the 25th (Lightning) Infantry Division in the Pacific. 'Don't stop men when they're moving,' he protested to Hodges. Instead he suggested that they should let the troops pass the fortifications around Aachen first and then pause so that fresh supplies could be brought up from the Normandy beach-heads. Wouldn't Hodges authorize a 'reconnaissance in force' for 13 September, in order to breach the Siegfried Line before the Germans had a chance to put troops into it?

In the end Hodges backed down. He told Collins and Gerow to go ahead with their advance towards Aachen. But he warned them that if they ran into 'solid opposition' and failed to achieve 'quick penetration', they were to halt and wait for further supplies.

Collins grinned but said nothing. In spite of everything he had his go-ahead. In his own mind he knew that once he had started his 'reconnaissance in force', he would soon develop it into a full-scale attack. Then he'd let General Hodges worry about keeping his VII Corps supplied.

That day Collins' 80,000-man VII Corps was located on a 35-mile front around and beyond Aachen. The country was difficult for his armour to operate in, not only because it was heavily fortified, but it was also thickly wooded and very hilly. However, there was a stretch of the surrounding countryside leading to the little town of Stolberg which was comparatively flat. This was the so-called 'Stolberg Corridor', which was to feature largely in the bitter fighting of the weeks to come.

In essence Collins decided that while the US Army's most

experienced infantry division, the First, nicknamed the 'Big Red One' after the divisional shoulder patch, which had fought on every American front since North Africa in 1942, probed forward in the direction of Aachen, General Maurice Rose's 3rd Armored Division, the 'Spearhead', would strike against the face of the Stolberg Corridor. Should these two divisions manage to breach the Siegfried Line defences, the 'Big Red One' were to rush Aachen, while Rose's Shermans would move forward, outflanking the city, taking Eschweiler and then on to Düren.

It was a bold plan, unknown in its full ramifications to either Hodges or Eisenhower, born of the easy confidence of that month, when it seemed that the 'Krauts' were on the run everywhere and that vaunted '1,000 year Reich' was about to crumble into ruins. Collins was soon to learn just how optimistic this view was.

All that day, his men moved up towards the front, ready for the big push of the morrow. In the Dutch town of Vaals just west of Aachen, the brothers Joep and Will Neus-Mommers placed two great baskets of fruit on either side of the road for the American infantry on their way up to the line. Greedily the GIs grabbed the pears, but the basket full of apples remained completely untouched. All that day not one soldier took an apple and the brothers shook their heads in wonder and asked themselves, 'Don't Americans like apples?'

In the Belgian town of Hergenrath, to the south of Aachen, German-born Lene Nellessen worried about her own fate as an 'enemy civilian' and that of her war-blind husband and two daughters, as she watched the Americans advance under a light artillery bombardment. When the bombardment stopped she decided to take her husband and children for a walk in the park. She did not get far. As she approached the park, the muzzle of a machine pistol was poked round a corner. 'Don't shoot, please,' she called in English, 'There are children here!'

Slowly the machine pistol was withdrawn and a moment later a big black GI came into view. He said casually, 'Nice day for a war, ain't it?'

The ice was broken. He offered the war-blinded veteran a cigarette. Herr Nellessen refused; he was a non-smoker. His wife was not so foolish. The cigarette would buy a few slices of bread on the black market. She accepted it gratefully, as did the children the chocolate, the first they'd seen for months, which the black soldier offered them. Then he went on his way.

In the little German hamlet of Schmithof Pastor Welter acted immediately when the villagers told him that the 'Amis' were approaching. In his robe, with the Host in one hand and a briefcase containing the church records and funds in the other, he went fearfully down the dusty road to meet them. The GIs were suspicious. They surrounded him, bayonets fixed to the muzzles of their rifles, while he tried to explain in German that there were no German soldiers in Schmithof. The hard expressions on their unshaven faces did not change; none of them had understood a word he had said! He tried again in French. This time one of the GIs understood. Hastily he explained that he was coming to surrender the hamlet. The Americans relaxed. Indeed a couple of them bent one knee and crossed themselves when he said he was bearing the Host. Then an officer pushed his way through the circle of GIs and thrust out his hand: 'Good day, Herr Pfarrer,' he said heartily in a mixture of English and German. 'Nice to be in Germany again!'

General Collins' Corps was in position for the great attack. Everything was working smoothly.

CHAPTER THREE

PANIC reigned in Aachen that day! Everywhere reports were flooding into the headquarters of General Schack, commander of the German 81st Corps and responsible for Aachen, that the enemy had penetrated all along the front in the Eifel; and it did not take him long to realize that their objective was Aachen.

Schack knew well that his four weak divisions, equipped with a handful of tanks salvaged from the débâcle in France, were no match for the Americans. All the same he realized that if the enemy concentrated on the city itself, they were playing into his hands in two ways. Aachen could well become the German 'Stalingrad', as indeed Goebbels was already promising the nation. Furthermore, Aachen was a symbol of Germanic greatness and played an important rôle in National Socialist mythology. Thus if Goebbels managed to involve the Americans in a battle for Aachen, not only would the advantage be on the side of the defenders, as it always is in such cases, but the emotional significance of that battle would compel the Führer to send him urgently needed reinforcements, which he would not otherwise receive.

In the end the General decided to send his best surviving division to Aachen. Under the command of Lieutenant-General Count Gerhard von Schwerin, the 116th 'Greyhound' Panzer Division would—with the assistance of three fortress battalions—be responsible for the defence of the city. Thus it fell to the lot of this ill-fated German aristocrat to participate in a battle which he did not wish to fight and which, before it was over, nearly cost him his life at the hands of a firing squad made up of his own countrymen.

Count von Schwerin was a professional soldier and had been responsible for the 'England-desk' in the German War Ministry before the war where he had become a personal friend of a British officer who was later to be Eisenhower's Chief-of-Intelligence, General Strong. Under his command the 116th Panzer had taken Sarajevo, cracked open the Uman Pocket, freed three other German divisions from a Russian trap and gained the reputation of being as fast and as brave as the greyhound which his men wore so proudly on the side of their peaked caps. Indeed in 1943, he had been the third general in the whole of the German Army to receive the Knight's Cross of the Iron Cross with oak leaves and swords. Hitler thought of him as a 'splendid battlefield commander who unfortunately was not a National Socialist'.

By 1944 von Schwerin was totally disillusioned with the Nazi régime. He knew of the July Plot to assassinate Hitler, for which one of his relatives, Count von Schwerin-Schwanenfeld, was later executed. Indeed if the Plot had succeeded, it was to have been von Schwerin who would approach the Allies on behalf of the rebellious Generals. But the assassination attempt failed and von Schwerin fought on for a cause in which he no longer believed.

This was the man whose staff car now nosed its way through the pathetic columns of ragged civilians being forced to evacuate Aachen at the command of the *Kreisleiter* Schmeer, who had already fled the city with most of the police and the rest of the National Socialist administration. The brown-shirted heroes, who only a few days before had been echoing Goebbels' shrilled boast that 'no enemy foot would ever enter Aachen', had 'evacuated' themselves to the safety of Jülich, leaving the inhabitants to fend for themselves as best they could.

Arriving at his HQ in the Hotel Quellenhof, General von Schwerin smiled ironically when told of the flight of the 'Golden Pheasants', as the Party officials were known on account of their addiction to gold braid and fancy uniforms. Although Goebbels had promised that Aachen would be defended by elite troops, on whom 'our enemies will break their teeth', he realized that apart from his own men, the city's defence consisted of what he called 'Christmas Tree soldiers'—old men, formed into 'stomach battalions' and 'ear and throat battalions',* and inexperienced youngsters. With such men he could achieve nothing save the senseless destruction of one of Germany's most noble cities. Already he realized that he could not maintain the front *south* of Aachen along the line of the *Aachener Wald;* instead he would have to form his line *north* of the city near Würselen. That would mean Aachen would be open for the taking.

'How many civilians are still here?' he asked.

'It's hard to say, sir. We estimate perhaps forty thousand.'

The General nodded. 'All right,' he ordered, 'make a public announcement that I, as battle commandant of Aachen, order that there will be no further attempt to evacuate the city. I believe the *Oberburgermeister* left an emergency administration behind. I want those people to report to me at once.'

Some of the staff officers looked shocked. After all, the

---

* Battalions made up exclusively of men suffering from these complaints, who could be given their special diets and treatments in handy groups.

order to evacuate the city, given originally by *Oberburger-meister* Janssen at the command of the Gauleiter of Cologne, came from the Führer himself. Hadn't the Führer stated that Aachen should be fought for to the end, even if it went down in ruins in the attempt?

Von Schwerin soon made it clear that he felt any defence of Aachen was useless. No one could expect it to stand up to a full-scale American attack, and already the enemy guns and dive-bombers were beginning the softening-up process, prior to starting their all-out offensive.

He ordered a poster to be prepared, to be displayed throughout the city, which declared his intention to surrender Aachen to the Americans without a fight. It ended with the words: 'If the city is taken by the enemy, avoid any action against them. Don't forget you are German! Maintain your honour as Germans, but don't undertake any action which would give the enemy cause to take reprisals.'

If that was not enough, the courageous General, who fully realized that he was taking his life in his hands by resisting Hitler's express order that Aachen should be defended to the last, went one step further. As the 12th gave way to the 13th, and the roar of the softening-up barrage grew ever louder and the remaining civilians began to plunder the shops, he wrote a personal note in English to the still unknown enemy commander. It read: 'I stopped the absurd evacuation of this town; therefore I am responsible for the fate of its inhabitants and I ask you in the case of an occupation by your troops to take care of the unfortunate population in a humane way. I am the last German Commanding Officer in the Sector of Aachen.

Schwerin'[*]

---

[*] The hastily pencilled original can still be seen in one of the city's museums.

Searching through the empty administration buildings, he found a minor postal official in one of the ruins and summoned him into an office. There he told him 'I've asked you to come here because I have a task for you upon which depends the future of your home town. I have a communication here which I want you to give to the first American officer who enters your office if the city is taken. Ask him to give it to his commanding officer at once. This letter will be decisive for the future of the local population. Do you realize your responsibility?'

The man nodded and von Schwerin dismissed him, satisfied that he had indeed saved one of Germany's most historical cities. Now, he knew, everything depended upon the Americans taking Aachen before General Schack received the reinforcements promised by the High Command, which would enable him to turn Charlemagne's city into a bloody battlefield.

If they didn't capture Aachen within the next twenty-four hours, not only would his own fate be sealed as a traitor to the National Socialist cause, but also that of the 40,000-odd Aacheners who now remained behind in the ruins at his own command. He had done all he could. The ball was in the Americans' court. Everything depended on the troops commanded by General Huebner, Commander of the 1st US Infantry Division, and by General Maurice Rose of the 3rd Armored.

CHAPTER FOUR

THE commander who was first to test the strength of the defences around Aachen bore the suitably heroic name of Leander. Lt-Colonel Leander Doan was commander of the 3rd Armored's Task Force X. As daylight broke on the morning of the 13th, Doan's mixed force of tanks and armoured infantry broke out of their laager and attacked a nest of pillboxes at the edge of a thick pine wood near Oberforstbach. In spite of heavy opposition from a mixed bag of old men and fanatical 17- and 18-year-olds, Leander Doan's 1,600-strong force made steady progress, breaking through the first barrier of dragon's teeth on the top of a steep wooded hill. Before them they could see the full extent of what they called the 'Scharnhorst Line' (a newer extension of the West Wall) stretching across the countryside to left and right.

But there was little time to view the scenery. Crouched in tight bunches behind the Shermans, they started to advance slowly and cautiously towards the enemy defensive positions.

Almost at once the enemy opened up with their 88mm cannon. Still the armoured infantry pressed on. The combat engineers, sweating on behind them, burdened by the weight of their explosive charges, started to destroy the first of the abandoned pillboxes. Suddenly one of the pillboxes, supposedly already knocked out, came to life again. Spandau fire sprayed the lines of infantry strung out behind the tanks.

Under the command of Captain Bill Plummer an infantry platoon rushed the enemy in their midst. The air was suddenly full of agonized cries of 'Medic, Medic!' But, in spite of their casualties, the infantry got closer and closer to the lone bunker which was defying the Spearhead Division.

Finally Plummer and a handful of his men made it to the bunker's 'blind side'. 'Come out and surrender!' he called.

'Go to hell!' a muffled voice called from within the pillbox in English.

Plummer hesitated no longer. He nodded to the engineer corporal carrying the satchel tetryl charges. 'Okay, corporal, take 'em!'

The soldier rushed forward, covered by the fire of his comrades. He thrust the high explosive through the nearest aperture and flung himself in a shell-hole. For a moment nothing happened. Then there was a muffled crump. Violet flame shot out of the aperture, followed by acrid yellow smoke. The pillbox heaved. Bits of concrete fell from its side. The firing ceased from within. The advance went on.

Farmer Wilhelm Maahsen prayed. Caught between the main German line of defence and the creeping American barrage, which was covering the infantry's advance, he prayed as he had never prayed before.

Outside, his shell-pitted fields were littered with his dead cows, while a couple of his plough-horses ran crazily from field to field whenever another shell came howling over towards the bunker-line. But still, he and his family, cowering in the cellar of his farmhouse, were as yet uninjured.

Farmer Maahsen had had trouble enough with the defensive line in these last six years. In 1938 he had been forced to leave his farm by the Nazis to help to build it; then when the enemy had started to approach the frontiers of the Reich, the SS had roused him out once more to dig trenches and machine gun nests for them. Every morning and evening he had passed through their positions and every time he had had trouble because, devout Catholic as he was, he had refused to say 'Heil Hitler!' Instead he had given the old Catholic greeting of 'Gruss Gott'.* After a while the SS had begun to call him 'Herr Gruss Gott', and made him wait anything up to another thirty minutes in the evening on his way home when all the rest of the conscripted labourers had long since vanished into the darkness.

With fervour but in silence, Farmer Maahsen promised himself that if he and his family ever got out of this terrible bombardment alive, he would build a little chapel on the heights above.†

By midday Colonel Leander Doan realized that he wasn't making the progress he had expected. Every time the attacking infantry broke through one enemy defensive position, they ran into another. Soon he knew the steam would go out of the doughboys and the attack would bog down. He would have to have a breakthrough soon.

Then Colonel Doan struck lucky. One of his recce patrols found a small cart track, which apparently had been built by the local farmers so that they could take their wagons through the dragon's teeth. The Colonel did not hesitate. He ordered his main armoured drive to switch its advance down the primitive track. But in spite of his eagerness, Doan still suspected a trap. The track was too good to be true. It

* Roughly 'Greet God'. To which the SS were wont to answer, 'Yes, when you see him.'
† He did.

might be mined! Just to be sure, he ordered a British-made Scorpion flail tank to lead the advance.

Sergeant Dahl, the commander of the Scorpion, drove cautiously down the dusty track, its great iron chains revolving noisily two yards in front of it, flailing the earth to explode any hidden mines. But nothing happened! The reconnaissance patrol had made a real find. There was no trap. The Germans had not mined the track.

But Sergeant Dahl's luck soon ran out. Suddenly the Scorpion came to an abrupt halt. By a hundred to one chance one of the chains had caught on the spike of one of the dragon's teeth and forced the tank to a stop! He barked out an order to his driver. The driver threw the Scorpion into reverse. Nothing happened! It would not budge. Then the worst happened—German artillery discovered the tank.

An 88mm cracked into angry life. The 100-pound shell ripped the air apart. Dahl did not wait for a second shell. He pulled off his throat mike and yelled 'Let's get the hell outa here!' His crew needed no urging. Together they abandoned the tank and ran to the rear, followed by German machine gun fire. The advance of the 3rd Armored Division had come to a halt, due to a minor technical hazard.

Meanwhile the US Army's premier infantry division, General Huebner's 'Big Red One', was also having its troubles. The Division's 16th Infantry Regiment, which was leading the advance, had run into one hitch after another in its advance from Belgium into Germany. Now, however, in the face of small-scale but determined counter-attacks, the Sixteenth's leading battalion had managed to penetrate into the Aachen *Staatsforst*.*

* One of the many woods surrounding the city.

In General Schack's HQ, the news that the *Amis* were so close to Aachen caused the greatest alarm. Schack telephoned von Schwerin immediately and ordered him to use his 116th Panzer to drive the Americans out of the forest at once before they had time to dig in.

The call put von Schwerin in a terrible quandary. He had sworn to himself that Aachen would not become another 'Stalingrad', as Goebbels had promised the German people it would. But now he had received a direct order from his superior to enter the battle for the city. What should he do? Should he obey his Corps Commander's orders, or should he wait and give the *Amis* the chance to take the place without a fight? In the end he compromised. He ordered his panzer grenadiers to counter-attack with the assistance of a few replacements and the self-propelled guns of the 34th Assault Gun Brigade, which were being hurriedly unloaded at Aachen's main station.

An hour or so later these troops had been able to force back the American 'point' and General von Schwerin could report to a relieved Schack that he had 'closed the gap south of Aachen'. All the same von Schwerin knew that there still were American infantry in the *Staatsforst* and he still had a chance of keeping his promise to make Aachen an open city, if only the damned *Amis* trying to break into the Stolberg Corridor would hurry up!

Although the light was already starting to go on this crucial 13 September, General Maurice Rose, the 3rd Armored Division's commander, was determined that he was going to break through the enemy defences.

Maurice Rose, a Rabbi's son who had worked himself up from private soldier to general, in spite of the prejudice against Jews in the pre-war Regular Army, was different from the usual run of American divisional commanders at that time. His former CO General Harmon described him once as a 'cool, able soldier, distant and removed in temperament and no one could know him well'. Rarely did he take into account the feelings or fears of his men. When he gave an order, he expected it to be carried out regardless of the cost. Now he commanded that the farm track leading through the Aachen defences had to be taken, come what may.

As a result, Sergeant Sverry Dahl was forced to brave the Kraut 88s yet again. Perched on the tank of his platoon commander, Lieutenant John R. Hoffmann, he directed the Sherman towards his stricken Scorpion. While the 88s pounded the fields all around them, Hoffmann's Sherman and that of his platoon sergeant hitched towing cables to the trapped Scorpion and finally managed to pull it free. Dahl waited no longer. Springing from the turret of Hoffmann's tank, he dashed towards his own tank. He started up. The Scorpion lurched forward, its flails whirling once more. The way was free!

Some way back along the track, Colonel Leander Doan made a decision. In spite of the fact that a tank was highly vulnerable at night—when some teenage Hitler Youth armed with a *panzerfaust** could knock out 20,000 dollars of expensive machinery and four or five highly trained men—Colonel Doan knew that General Rose would not accept the darkness and the dangers it brought as an excuse for not pushing on.† He ordered his Task Force to continue the advance, slip-

* The German bazooka.
† Six months later General Rose himself was killed in Germany because he insisted on advancing at night in his tanks and because he had not accepted General Harmon's dictate that a CO should not ride at the point during an advance. Trapped with a small force of tankers

ping in a further twenty Shermans behind the Scorpion. Thus as Dahl drew his tank to one side to let the 30-ton monsters clank by, Task Force X began to disappear into the growing gloom. But by now the defenders had been warned. They were waiting!

What Colonel Doan feared might happen, happened. German soldiers popped up from the ditches on both sides of the track. There was a sharp crack, followed by a stab of scarlet flame. The rocket flew through the darkness, followed by a shower of fiery sparks. The hollow boom of metal striking metal. The first *panzerfaust* hit home, and the lead tank lurched to a halt.

Within the next five minutes, Doan lost four Shermans. Sitting ducks as they were on the narrow track, they were struck one after another, blue smoke pouring from their highly inflammable gasoline engines. Now their crews were flinging themselves out of the turrets and escape hatches and running madly to the rear, followed by the angry zigzag of tracer bullets.

But the punishment of Doan's Task Force for being so foolhardy as to advance at night without covering infantry did not end there. The guns of the 34th Assault Gun Brigade had now reached the front. The huge Ferdinands, armed with cannon almost twice as powerful as those of the undergunned Shermans, thundered into action. The night was hideous with the roar of their cannon. Within fifteen minutes of their arrival on the scene Doan lost another six tanks. Desperately he pushed on. But it was no use. The track behind the lead tank was now littered with burning,

near Paderborn, Rose attempted to surrender to a group of SS men. Mistaking his action, when he tried to unbuckle his shoulder holster, an SS let him have a burst from a machine pistol and killed him. The post-war inquiry showed that it was a genuine mistake.

wrecked Shermans. In the end Doan gave up. With only ten
Shermans left, he ordered his men to stop and dig in for the
night. The 3rd Armored's advance had come to a halt. Aachen would not be taken that day. Wednesday, 13 September, 1944 had proved to be decidedly unlucky for General
Collins.

CHAPTER FIVE

On the night of Wednesday, 13 September, General von Schwerin was a very worried man. Twenty-four hours had passed since he had written his note in English to the American commander, offering to surrender Aachen, and still the Americans had not appeared. Where the devil were they? All that night he paced the floor of his operations room in his new HQ, in a farmhouse near the village of Berensberg, wondering what he should do next and waiting for the Americans to arrive.

Dawn came on Thursday, grey and cold. Still no Americans. Just before breakfast the General received a radio signal transmitted by Schack from the Führer's own HQ. It read, 'Aachen has to be evacuated. If necessary use force.* Only fighting troops to be left in the city.'

Von Schwerin gave in. He had no other choice. Since the attempt on his life in July, Hitler tolerated no disobedience from his generals. Rebellious generals had been slowly garroted with a piece of piano wire and aged field-marshals hung up by a butcher's hook thrust through their jaws. Sad at heart, von Schwerin rescinded his original order. The useless evacuation began once again.

There was worse to come. On the morning of Friday, 15 September, Cremer, the deputy head of the emergency city administration, was arrested in his bed by the Gestapo, and hurried off to prison in nearby Cologne. That same after-

* i.e. against any civilian who attempted to remain behind.

noon, the rest of the emergency administration met in the Hotel Quellenhof. But their meeting did not get very far. With the Gestapo suddenly sealing off the Hotel's exits and entrances, the main door opened to reveal no less a person than *Kreisleiter* Schmeer, the local party leader, who had fled so hurriedly a few days before. The Nazi Party had returned to Aachen.*

Now special units of the Storm Troops, the SA 'Old Guard', began to flood into the city to ensure that the civilians carried out Hitler's order to evacuate it. Under the command of a fanatical Berlin SA officer named Major Zimmermann, they swiftly set the long sad treks moving eastwards again. They forced the frightened civilians out of the cellars and ruins where they were hiding, driving them to the assembly areas like so many cattle. As the bombastic Major announced to the emergency administration: 'Only those people may remain in Aachen who have a place in the coming battle. Everything else is ballast. Everything else must be moved—*without mercy!*'

Count von Schwerin spent a long, nerve-wracking day wondering whether his compromising letter had been discovered. Then the bombshell dropped. On the morning of 16 September General Schack telephoned him personally. 'Schwerin,' he told him sadly, 'it can be only a matter of hours now before you are relieved of your command. Please place yourself at my disposal.' Without another word the Corps Commander hung up.

But von Schwerin knew all he wanted to know. His letter had been found. He slumped down on his wooden chair in

---

* The sudden return didn't save Schmeer. Angered by the way he had fled from Aachen, Hitler ordered that Schmeer be stripped of his Party office and sent to the front as an infantry private. That was the last that was heard of him.

Above: Dragonsteeth, Siegfried Line, West Wall: the three names given to the protective concrete wall on the border of the German Reich. It was meant to impede the enemy's artillery, but this objective was scarcely fulfilled. *Below left:* He was meant to break through the West Wall at Aachen: the Commander of the 7th U.S. Corps, Major-General J. Lawton Collins ("Lightning Joe"). *Below right:* Lieutenant-General Friedrich August Schack, Commander of the 81st Army Corps.

The "Hanging Teddy Bear" and the U.S. foot soldier. In the background is the Käfer Restaurant (at Eschweiler?).

Above: Frans Hermans (left) and Fritz Eygelshoven, 1974, in the Dutch border village of Rimburg. In 1944, the then 20-year-old Fritz lost his left arm owing to a shrapnel wound.

Right: This man, Major-General Clarence R. Huebner, Commander of the 1st U.S. Infantry Division (the "Big Red One") liked to drill his soldiers strictly.

Above: A street fight in October, 1944: Americans carry an injured comrade to a doorway on the Von-Pastor-Platz. In the background is a Sherman tank. *Below:* The place where the last SS troops made their last stand was the cellar of the Aachen house, 7 Weyhestrasse (then 17). In front of the two cellar windows is Peter Schaaf, 49. In 1944, as a member of the SS Battalion Rink, he lay in this cellar.

the humble farmhouse kitchen which served as his ops room, head sunk between his hands. He, whose family had served the German state for generations, would now be dragged in front of the feared 'People's Court' like a common criminal. Now he had nothing to look forward to but torture, disgrace and a hideous lingering death, suspended by a piece of chicken wire from a hook in some Gestapo cellar. The game was up. He was finished. But General von Schwerin had not reckoned with the loyalty of the men of his 'Greyhound' Division.

On Sunday, 17 September, he drove to General Schack's HQ. His Corps Commander got down to business straightaway. 'At the supreme command of Field-Marshal Model,' he told von Schwerin, 'I have orders to arrest you at once and deliver you to the nearest People's Court attached to the Seventh Army HQ at Munstereifel.' Schwerin tried to play for time. 'All right,' he replied, 'but I would at least like to have time to take my leave from my "Greyhounds".'

Schack nodded. 'Very well. You can return to your Division now. But after that you must return here at once. Understood?'

'Understood.'

By this time, however, the news of their General's impending arrest had penetrated to the rank and file of the Division. They were enraged. They discussed the matter among themselves as they waited in the ruined suburbs for the *Amis* to come. 'Why should he take the blame for the Golden Pheasants when they were responsible for the evacuation? After all he didn't run away. They did!'

But his men's reaction was not limited to the usual grumbling. A squadron of tanks began to block the roads to Düren and Jülich, where elements of the premier SS division, the *Leibstandarte* (Adolf Hitler's Bodyguard Division), were stationed. If the SS men tried to snatch the commander of the 116th Panzer, these troopers intended to stop them—by force if necessary. In addition, a motor-cycle troop of experienced panzer grenadiers attached themselves to the General himself as a personal bodyguard, determined to sacrifice their own lives for his.

Von Schwerin saw the way the wind was blowing and made his decision. Although he would hand his division over to his senior regimental commander, he would disobey the order to return to Munstereifel. Instead he would remain at his farmhouse HQ and wait for the *Amis* to overrun Aachen; then he would surrender himself and his devoted 'Greyhounds' to them.

On that same sunny Friday which had marked the return of the Party to the besieged city, General Rose ordered his Combat Command B to carry on from where the ill-fated Task Force X had left off. Under the command of Lieutenant-Colonel William Lovelady, the CCB would now head the 3rd Armored Division's main push into the Stolberg Corridor. As the day progressed Lovelady's tanks crossed the Vicht River, south of Stolberg, over a bridge the Germans had failed to blow up, and pushed forward rapidly. By eleven o'clock progress was still excellent and Lovelady was pleased. One hour later his lead Shermans were two miles beyond the river and were already passing the first line of German fortifications, abandoned by their frightened middle-aged defenders.

Now the 'point' was advancing cautiously along the highway between the villages of Mausbach and Gressnich, which lay in a narrow valley, but with open grassy spaces on both sides of the road. The reason for the column's slowness was that the experienced commander of the lead tank knew that this was ideal country for anti-tank gunners. He ordered his driver to slow down even further. Three hundred yards behind him the cover Sherman did the same. Now the two tanks were just crawling along. The crews were tense and sweating. Yard by yard they crawled up the deserted, battle-littered road. Still nothing happened. Then, just as the leading Sherman reached a kilometre stone, half-way between the two villages, six German self-propelled guns appeared to their right. Before the Americans could react, the leading Ferdinand cracked into action. The Sherman reeled and an instant later thick white smoke started to pour from it. The crew abandoned it at once. The shell had struck near the gasoline engine and it wasn't for nothing that the Shermans were nicknamed 'Ronsons'; their engines often burst into flames when just one of the rear sprockets was struck by a shell. The frightened tankers ran for the cover of the nearest ditch.

Now the Ferdinands, which had routed the leading patrols of the 'Big Red One' in the *Staatsforst*, began to work the Shermans over. Although the Sherman gunners could fire six shells for every one fired by the Ferdinand gunners, the armour of the American tanks could not stand up to the tremendous punch of the German cannon. In rapid succession seven Shermans were knocked out. An American tank-destroyer tried to tackle the massed Ferdinands. It didn't get far. A German shell struck its front sprocket. The M-3 reared up on its tracks like a wild horse. When it came down again, its gun was silent. Behind it on the road, an ambulance carrying wounded tankers was hit. It skidded to a halt, its windscreen shattered, its front tyres burst, scattering wounded everywhere. Those who were still alive crawled for safety with painful slowness, leaving a trail of blood behind them.

In the end Colonel Lovelady gave in. The 3rd Armored's drive was over for that day. The Germans had stopped the Division yet again. Reluctantly he ordered the survivors to pull back to the village of Mausbach and take up a defensive position. There he contacted General Rose by radio and told him what had happened; he had only thirteen tanks left. He had lost nearly 60% of the tanks authorized for a 2,000-man strong combat command. Reluctantly, knowing Rose's cold unfeeling attitude towards human life *and* his hot temper, he asked permission to halt for the night.

General Rose's reply is not recorded; he was always intolerant of failure and in the months to come he would recommend more than one field grade officer to be court-martialled for cowardice when he failed to take an objective (notably during the Battle of the Bulge). But in the end he allowed a worried Lovelady to remain where he was. But only for the time being; General Maurice Rose had new plans for the morrow.

Meanwhile the situation on the other side of the line was not much better. Earlier that day, General Schack had called General Mueller, CO of the weak 9th Panzer Division, who had successfully held the 3rd Armored with the aid of the Ferdinands at Mausbach, and ordered him 'to attack the enemy and throw him back behind the West Wall. There is no time to lose!'

So Mueller threw in his inexperienced, young panzer grenadiers. Advancing as if they were on parade, they attacked the American positions at Zweifall. The American artillery pulverized them and they fled. But their officers rallied them and they went in again. The barrage stopped them once more. Three times they attacked and three times they were thrown back, leaving the shell-holed fields littered with their corpses. They did not attack a fourth time.

When he heard the news, Schack, who was soon to be relieved on account of his 'lack of fighting spirit', nearly broke down. He knew the Americans would attack again on the morrow and this time Mueller's 9th, after the terrible punishment it had taken at Zweifall, would not be able to hold them. The Stolberg Corridor would be wide open. Just then an aide called him to the 'phone. It was 7th Army HQ. The Führer had personally ordered the release of the 12th Infantry Division, presently refitting in East Prussia, to his weak Corps. Under its new commander, Colonel Gerhard Engel, an ambitious 38-year-old officer, who had won the Knight's Cross in Russia and had recently served on Hitler's staff as an adjutant, the 12th Infantry Division numbered nearly 15,000 young men, had an anti-tank battalion and its full complement of artillery, plus seventeen assault guns. Its first contingents were scheduled to reach nearby Düren and Jülich that very night, with the rest of the Division to follow within the next thirty hours.

As General Schack put down the 'phone, he felt an overwhelming sense of relief. A fresh division was coming under his command, led by a man appointed by Hitler himself and with the Führer's ear; there would be plenty of material support at the highest level.

As the front began to settle down for another night, General Schack saw that when his opponent attacked on the morrow, he could well be walking into a trap. The only problem now was, 'Would Colonel Engel and his Division arrive in time?'

CHAPTER SIX

On the morning of the 16th, General Rose's 3rd Armored Division struck yet another bunker line. Although it was manned by middle-aged soldiers of one of Schack's stomach battalions, they still managed to slow down the advancing tankers. Later the US Army newspaper *The Stars and Stripes* would make a good story out of the captured defenders of that line, calling them 'stomach cases, cripples with glass eyes and wooden legs'.

But the harassed infantry attacking the bunkers did not think the defenders one bit funny. As one of them remarked bitterly: 'I don't care if the guy behind that gun is a syphilitic prick who's a hundred years old—he's still sitting behind eight feet of concrete and he's still got enough fingers to press triggers and shoot bullets.' The combat engineers were called up to try and blast a way through the line. But the men were unused to this kind of work; these were the first bunkers they had ever tackled. As Corporal Frederick Griffin of Company A recalled: 'The first time we put twenty packs of tetryl inside and let her go. She (the bunker) went up in the air, turned a half flip and came down. After that we used less and less. It all depends how big and thick it is.'

But that wasn't the end of the engineers' problems, as Corporal Griffin remembers: 'When we were in a big hurry, we sometimes blew up only certain ones so that we'd break the chain and they couldn't cover each other even if the

Krauts did get back. Lots of these pillboxes weren't manned and we never knew which was which, especially if the infantry bypassed them. That bothered the hell out of us because when we're loaded with tetryl like that and a shell lands anywhere near us, there isn't enough left of us even to make a good memory.'

That Saturday a lot of tankers and engineers became just a faint memory!

Still General Rose persisted in his attack, despite growing losses. Driving from frontline command to command, dressed in a gleaming lacquered helmet with twin silver stars, beige riding breeches and gleaming custom-made boots, he urged his flagging commanders on to ever greater efforts.

At the village of Geisberg, his massed Shermans easily beat off a local German counter-attack with their long 75mms. Nevertheless when, at Rose's command, his Shermans and their supporting infantry tried to push into the northern suburbs of Stolberg itself, they were brought to a complete stop by intense artillery and small arms fire. Rose allowed the local commander there to dig in among the ruins and ordered the direction of the attack to be changed. His armour now tried to capture Weissenberg, attacking from the village of Gressnich. For a time they were successful, but in the end the attack petered out as they failed to capture a wrecked factory which dominated the hill to the southwest of Weissenberg. Again Rose had been stalled.

While Schack's Corps fought back desperately, trying to win time until the 12th Infantry Division arrived, General Rose decided to intervene in the battle personally. It was only four more hours to darkness and there was a four-mile gap between his two stalled combat commands into which some aggressive German commander could slip at will—and that was something that Rose was not going to let happen! Scratching together what he could find in the way of infantry and attaching to them his sole remaining tank reserve, he flung the hastily organized force into an attack on the high ground near Buesbach at the south-eastern end of Stolberg.

Once again the guns thundered. Behind the rolling barrage, the Shermans started to crawl forward, each followed by little groups of infantry, plodding towards the silent enemy positions, sweating hands gripping their weapons, eyes wide, shoulders bent like farmers pushing a plough.

One hundred yards, two hundred, still the unseen German defenders did not open fire. Two hundred and fifty. Now the barrage had swept over the German front and died away altogether. Three hundred yards. They could see the new, brown earth of the German positions now. The Shermans speeded up, engines roaring, their tracks showering the men behind them with mud and pebbles. The infantry began to run awkwardly over the uneven ground. A minute more and they would be there.

Then it happened. There was the familiar, terrifying, high-pitched burr of the German MG 42. Everywhere GIs pitched to the ground and the agonized cry for the 'medics' rose from the wounded. Officers blew their whistles. NCOs bellowed orders. The survivors ran on, screaming hysterically. The slaughter began once again.

By nightfall Rose had closed the gap between his bogged-down combat commands. But the cost had been high. The exhausted survivors, slumped in foxholes or among the ruins of the suburbs, ate their suppers prior to bedding down for the night, knowing, as soldiers always do, that the morrow would be no better than today.

But not many of them were fated to get much sleep that

night. As soon as it grew dark and the Germans knew they were in no danger from the Allied Air Forces, the silence was disturbed by the faint roar of many motors coming from the east and getting closer all the time. The weary GIs sat up in their bedrolls and stared at each other in bewilderment.

Just after midnight a patrol from the Big Red One's 16th Infantry returned to their battalion CP and reported that they had been out scouting near the village of Eilendorf when they had spotted enemy troops approaching the village of Verlautenheide in columns of two's, reaching 'as far as the eye can see!'

Colonel Engel's 12th Infantry Division had arrived. The 'Wild Buffaloes', as they called themselves, had reached the Stolberg front just in time!

When the Americans had first crossed the German frontier nearly a week before, *General der Panzertruppe* Erich Brandenberger, the Commander of the Seventh German Army, defending the long front between Trier and Aachen, had thought that the situation was hopeless. With the men at his disposal, he felt, it was impossible to defend the 100-mile long frontier successfully. In his opinion, there was only one thing to do—retreat to the line of the Rhine. Now, seven days later, the promise of two new divisions, one of them the 12th Infantry commanded by a former adjutant of the Führer himself, filled him with new hope.

That Saturday night, he composed an order-of-the-day at his HQ in Munstereifel which read: 'The Seventh Army will defend its positions . . . and the West Wall to the last man and the last bullet. The penetrations achieved by the enemy will be recaptured. The forward line of bunkers will be regained.' And it was clear to the Army Commander who

would carry out that task of recapturing the lost bunker line
—Colonel Engel's 12th Infantry.

The 12th had an excellent reputation, having gained its
nickname, the 'Wild Buffaloes', from its exploits in Russia in
1941 when it had marched and fought its way from the old
East Prussian frontier with Russia right up to the source of
the Volga, 'sweeping everything in front of it like a herd of
wild buffaloes'. But naturally there were very few of the
original 'Wild Buffaloes' left now. Most of the rank-and-file
were young men called up in late 1942 or the early summer
of 1943 with very little combat experience. All the same,
most of the officers and many of the senior NCOs were veterans of the war in Russia. As long as they were in control,
Brandenberger reckoned, the Division would do well. But
he made one proviso to Schack: the 12th Infantry was not to
be flung into its first battle against the Americans in bits and
pieces. It must go into action as a complete unit. Schack had
promised the Army Commander that he would personally
ensure that this would take place.

But the events of that Saturday had obliged Schack to
break his promise. Rose's advance was becoming too dangerous. When the young men of the 1st Battalion of Engel's
27th Fusilier Regiment started to get out of the troop train
at Jülich, they found Schack's staff officers already waiting
for them. Before they realized what was happening, they
were marching to the front at Verlautenheide, north of Eilendorf. An hour later the 2nd Battalion arrived at the same
station to be met with urgent orders to march to Stolberg to
stop the 3rd Armored's push there. Just before dawn that
Sunday, two more of Engel's regiments started to detrain at
the railhead to be told that they were going into action immediately. They were ordered to attack the 3rd Armored's

point at the villages of Weissenberg and Mausbach and
drive the *Amis* back the way they had come.

Thus, within minutes of their arrival, Colonel Engel's division was split up all over the place and the young officer,
proud of his first divisional command, found he was rapidly
losing complete control of it. By dawn that Sunday, 17 September, the old Prussian military axiom of '*klotzen nicht
kleckern*'* had already been abandoned by General Schack,
in spite of Brandenberger's express order to the contrary,
and Colonel Engel's eager young men were to pay for it
with their lives.

The Fusiliers signalled their approach at Eilendorf with a
heavy artillery barrage which kept the GIs at the bottom of
their foxholes. When it ceased, the men of the 27th Fusilier
Regiment charged out of the woods between Verlautenheide and Stolberg in well-disciplined waves. They made
a perfect target for the veterans of the 3rd Armored. They
signalled back for artillery and mortar support. The American 'Long Toms'—155mm cannon with a range of over five
miles—cracked into action almost at once. Seconds later the
heavy mortar companies opened up. Suddenly the air was
full of the howl of mortar shells. They fell directly among
the ranks of the charging infantry who went down by the
score. Great gaps appeared among the first line. Still they
came on, only to be cut down by the fire of the men dug in
in the foxhole line.

Again and again, the Fusiliers tried to penetrate the
American line. But it was to no avail. The 3rd Armored
flung them back time after time. By noon the shell-cratered
fields in front of the Armored's positions were littered with

---

* The British military equivalent is roughly: 'Don't put your men in
penny packets'.

the dead and dying bodies of the 'Wild Buffaloes'. The total cost to the Americans was two dead and twenty-two wounded.

At Weissenberg the 48th Grenadier Regiment had better luck. Just as the Third was beginning its morning attack on the factory holding up the advance on the slope overlooking the village, the Grenadiers hit them head on. The Americans were caught off guard, out in the open. One Sherman was hit, then another. In the rear the armoured infantry started to drop. They began to waver. Slowly but surely the Grenadiers pushed the Americans down the slope.

General Rose was worried when he heard the news of the German success and decided to throw in his last reserves. Now the divisional barrel was empty. Still the Grenadiers pushed on. All morning the battle swayed back and forth. Finally, in the early afternoon it came to a halt. But when it did, the Grenadiers had recaptured virtually all the ground taken by the Third the day before.

The rest of the 48th Grenadier Regiment, which Schack had ordered to take the ground lost to the 3rd Armored near the village of Schevenhuette, ran into a trap. At mid-morning, an American patrol under Staff-Sergeant Harold Hellerich was cautiously checking out the ground in front of Schevenhuette when they spotted German infantry moving towards the village of Gressnich. Hellerich acted swiftly. Calling his company commander on his walkie-talkie, he told him what he had seen and then volunteered to observe the Germans until they entered the open fields ahead. When they were out in the open, he would call down the full weight of the 3rd Division's artillery on them. The company commander agreed to the plan and Sergeant Hellerich and his men took up their positions in the undergrowth.

Unsuspectingly, the young Grenadiers advanced boldly through the trees, watched by the little patrol, not knowing that each step they took was one closer to death. Confidently the first of them entered the fields. Hellerich could see how new their uniforms and equipment were. Obviously they were a green outfit. He began to count. There seemed to be four or five hundred men advancing across the fields—perhaps two companies. It was time to act.

'All right,' he said low. 'Stand by.' Hellerich placed the walkie-talkie to the right side of his face. 'They're here, sir,' he whispered to his company commander. 'Now . . . *FIRE!*'

The ragged crackle of small arms fire broke the stillness. A German pitched to the ground. Another cried out in agony as he was struck. The leading Grenadiers went to ground, just as Hellerich had hoped they would. He got on to his company commander again and called down the Third's artillery.

What happened next was not war, but sheer murder. Helpless, caught out in the open with absolutely no cover, the inexperienced young soldiers were slaughtered mercilessly. When that terrible bombardment ceased and the smoke of war started to drift away, a sight of stark brutality was revealed. The fields were littered with the shattered corpses of the Grenadiers. Later when American officers came out to count them, they estimated of the two companies who had entered the fields, only ten men had managed to escape. The slaughter of the 'Wild Buffaloes' had begun.

That dreadful Sunday afternoon, while the American artillery pounded the 12th Infantry Division remorselessly, Colonel Engel realized that his first day as a divisional commander had been a bitter failure. His young Division was

suffering tremendous casualties everywhere. As the sad survivors of one battalion, which had descended so confidently
from the troop train a mere twelve hours before, started to
straggle back across the battlefield to report their casualties,
Engel learned that they had lost 400 men killed or wounded.
Within those few short hours, the Battalion had lost four-
fifths of its strength! By evening he had had enough. He
telephoned to Schack. Feeling that the Corps Commander
had thrust his inexperienced men too hurriedly into the line
and had scattered their efforts in un-coordinated attacks
Engel asked—almost demanded—permission to postpone any
further attacks until he could re-organize his shattered
troops and prepare a concentrated attack.

In a hushed voice Schack gave his permission. He knew
that Engel enjoyed the Führer's favour and that his own
days as a Corps Commander were numbered; there was
nothing else he could do. The 12th Infantry could break off
the action and dig in for the night.

As he put down the 'phone, Schack knew in his heart that
his decision had virtually sealed the fate of Aachen. On the
morrow the *Amis* would surely attack again in force, unhin-
dered now by the only fresh troops he possessed. When they
did, nothing would be able to stop them.

The front began to settle down for the night. But Schack
could not sleep, for now he knew the city would not survive
another twenty-four hours once the enemy attack got underway. Aachen was nearly finished now.

CHAPTER SEVEN

MONDAY, 18 September dawned grey and chill. Everywhere the battered defenders of Aachen stood to and waited for the *Amis* to come for the last attack. But they waited in vain. The American line remained silent. That Sunday an event had taken place a hundred miles away in Holland which was to give Schack a week's grace before the Americans attacked in force again.

Just after midday on the 17th a great armada of British and American planes came roaring in to drop their loads. Along a sixty-mile stretch of Dutch countryside from Eindhoven to Arnhem, three divisions of British and American paratroopers had jumped from their Halifaxes and Dakotas, filling the sky with their red, white and green 'chutes. Field-Marshal Montgomery's bold plan to 'bounce' his troops across the Meuse and the Lower Rhine, thus swinging around the edge of the West Wall and thrusting deep into the Ruhr had begun.

The reaction of the US Army's overall land commander, General Omar Bradley, to the announcement of Montgomery's plan, code-named 'Market Garden', was: 'Had the pious, teetotaller Montgomery wobbled into SHAEF (Supreme Headquarters) with a hangover, I could not have been more astonished than I was by the daring adventure he proposed! For, in contrast to the conservative tactics

Montgomery ordinarily chose, the Arnhem attack was to be made over a sixty-mile carpet of airborne troops.'*

Although Bradley, who heartily disliked the British Field-Marshal, thought the Arnhem plan 'one of the most imaginative of the war', he telephoned General Eisenhower and 'objected strenuously to it'. Not only did he fear privately that Montgomery might win all the kudos of the final battle for Germany and the right to the ultimate prize of Berlin, leaving him out in the cold, he was also greatly worried as to how the British plan might affect his armies, in particular the supplies for his 1st and 3rd Armies.

But Eisenhower 'silenced my objections', Bradley wrote later. 'He thought the plan a fair gamble. It might enable us to outflank the Siegfried Line (West Wall), perhaps even snatch a Rhine River bridgehead.' But the crunch came at the end of the telephone conversation. Eisenhower ordained that in order to ensure that Montgomery's plan had the best possible chance of succeeding, the drive to Arnhem would have first priority in the way of supplies, which were being brought all the way from the Normandy beach-heads. (Although the Allies had been in France since 6 June, they still did not have a major port in operation.) To supply his British Second Army, under normal circumstances, Montgomery needed an air lift of 1,000 tons daily to the forward transport fields at Douai and Brussels and twelve times that amount brought up by road from Bayeux, his main supply base some 300 miles away. Now, in addition, he would need extra supplies to support a major, all-out offensive by the

* Market Garden envisaged the paras seizing three major bridges over the Lower Rhine and Meuse at Eindhoven, Nyjmegen and Arnhem until the British 2nd Army fought its way through the German front to link up with the most advanced force—the British 1st Para Division —holding the bridge at Arnhem.

2nd Army if it were to succeed in reaching the airborne men dropped so far ahead, deep behind enemy lines. In other words, Montgomery would get the supplies; Hodges' Army attacking through the Aachen Gap and Patton's through the Metz Gap wouldn't!

The lack of supplies was the writing on the wall for Joe Collins, when the news of Market Garden reached him on Sunday, the 17th. That and the appearance of Engel's 12th Infantry Division.

After a week of fighting on Germany's frontiers the US 1st Army had suffered 20,000 casualties and penetrated a mere twelve miles into the Reich. Some outfits had lost all their officers and many of their senior NCOs. Many units were being padded out with new men, raised from rearline outfits —military policemen, Army Air Corps men, anti-aircraft gunners and the like. In one infantry battalion, for instance, there was only one rifleman who knew how to use a flame-thrower. Soon Eisenhower would be forced to make a 5% levy on his rearline units to find sufficient men to fill the gaps in the First's battered frontline battalions. The 'canteen commandos', as they were called, would have to learn what real war was.

Sadly Collins realized that his first attempt to capture Aachen by 'a reconnaissance in force' had definitely failed. Looking back after the war, he reflected that 'a combination of things stopped us. We ran out of gas—that is to say we weren't completely dry, but the effect was much the same; we ran out of ammunition; and we ran out of weather. The loss of our tactical air support because of weather was a real blow.'

Thus after seven days of battle, silence fell upon the shell-shattered city. For the time being Aachen had been spared.

As silence fell over the front, a heavily armed SS patrol, led by an *Obersturmbannführer,* tried to break through the cordon set up by von Schwerin's 'Greyhounds' on the road to Düren. But the men of the 116th Panzer would not let the SS tankers through. They knew the SS men were after von Schwerin. The flushed *Obersturmbannführer* cried, 'Let me through! I've a special assignment.'

The officer in charge of the cordon remained unmoved by the SS Major's rage. Behind him his men were already training the cannon of their Mark IVs on the SS vehicles. If it came to a showdown, they would not hesitate to fire and he knew who would win. 'I've strict orders, *Obersturmbannführer,*' he replied calmly, 'not to let anyone without a written order into our section of the front. And I am empowered to defend my position with my weapons if necessary. I can't let you through.'

The *Obersturmbannführer* demanded the officer's name and grade. But in the end he turned his column about, muttering that the grinning panzer men would 'pay for this'.

Then General Schack took a hand. He called General von Schwerin's staff and told the senior officer: 'You must find the general at all costs. If necessary, I am prepared to come to Aachen personally and discuss this matter with him.'

Through an intermediary von Schwerin agreed to meet Schack at his former HQ in the Berensberg farmhouse. Schack turned up on time to find that von Schwerin was not there. He waited for half an hour and then realized that von Schwerin had stood him up. Concealing his anger as best he could, he returned to his Corps HQ without having seen the missing divisional commander.

Two hours later a heavily armed group of military and civilian policemen appeared in the farmyard. The rain had drowned the noise of their vehicles. Just in time von

Schwerin's batman warned him of the sudden appearance of the hated 'chained dogs'.* Hurriedly he escaped through a back window and was taken to Aachen by one of his loyal motor-cycle escort. There he 'went underground' in a little house in the *Kupferstrasse*, guarded by his men who occupied the shattered stairwell.

As the American guns remained obstinately silent and it became clear that the enemy had broken off his offensive, von Schwerin knew he could not remain in hiding much longer. After all, he was also risking the lives of his loyal 'Greyhounds' guarding him. Finally he decided to discuss the matter with his successor at the head of the 116th Panzer Division, Colonel Voigtsberger, who, unknown to both men, had already been denounced by the enraged *Obersturmbannführer* as 'that traitor von Schwerin's accomplice'. At that last meeting, von Schwerin decided he couldn't go on; he would have to surrender himself to the authorities.

Convinced that he was going to his death, *General-leutnant* von Schwerin gave himself up at General Brandenberger's HQ, located in the *Führerbunker†* in the woods east of Munstereifel. Here he was met by a sour-faced major, who escorted him to Field-Marshal von Rundstedt's HQ at Koblenz. Just before they left on their two-hour trip, the major warned the General firmly: '*Herr General,* if you attempt to flee, I shall be forced to shoot you.'

Von Schwerin nodded his understanding. In silence he walked to the car. A few minutes later they were on their

* MPs were known as 'chained dogs' because of the silver crescent plate which they wore on a chain round their necks.

† A specially constructed underground bunker complex, from which Hitler had directed the 1940 campaign against France.

way, followed, at a suitable distance, by a reconnaissance
troop of the 116th Panzer. Von Schwerin's 'Greyhounds'
were going to remain loyal to him to the end!*

Now the ruined city seemed abandoned to the middle-
aged, shabby 'field-greys' of the fortress companies. But
there was life enough below the ruins. Between five and ten
thousand civilians were still hiding out in Aachen's cellars,
in spite of the two forced evacuations. Wilhelm Savelsberg,
a 53-year-old former Aachen tram-driver, with his wife,
daughter-in-law, a small child and Emma, a small sheep,
was hiding out in the cellar of a ruined building in Aachen
at Number 104 *Auf der Hoernstrasse*. During that third
week of September, Savelsberg collected a small menagerie
of stray animals: chickens, ducks, geese, a turkey, even a
cow, which he kept hidden in a nearby shed and milked at
dead of night. But the Savelsbergs could not stay underground all the time. There was a young baby in the family
and its nappies wouldn't dry in the cellar. Thus the women
had to venture above ground to hang their washing in the
shattered upper storey of the house. That involved a twofold
danger: from the SA patrols still looking for civilians who
had refused to be evacuated and had gone into hiding, and
from American artillery. To appease the Americans, at least,
the two women decided to hang out a white flag in the

* Surprisingly enough, von Schwerin was freed. After a short trial,
he was released with 'a severe warning' probably due to the influence
of von Rundstedt. In December he was given a new division, the 90th
Panzergrenadier, and in 1945 the 76th Panzer Corps. Captured by the
British in April, 1945, his old friend General Strong had him brought
to Eisenhower's HQ at Reims to persuade him to go on a mission for
the Allies to Admiral Doenitz, the last German 'Führer'. Von Schwerin
refused. As he told Strong: 'I'm too well known as a non-Nazi. They'd
arrest me as a spy at once.'

upper storey, believing somewhat naïvely that if the enemy spotted it, they wouldn't fire.

Unfortunately one morning, just as the two of them had stolen upstairs to dry their washing, the white flag was spotted not by the Americans but by two wandering German artillerymen. Angrily they shouted up to the startled women, 'Get that damned white flag down at once!'

Frau Savelsberg refused. 'The *Amis* are close enough,' she retorted. 'We've got to protect ourselves.' 'All right,' the bigger of the two artillerymen shouted. 'Have it your own way. But tomorrow I'll see that the police collect you two.' And with that they went on their way, muttering something about having the 'pair of *Ami*-whores shot'.

Wilhelm Savelsberg, who had been hiding in the cellar, followed their progress with alarm. Would they really report his family to the police? He knew what that could mean— imprisonment for the women and the firing squad for himself. Just then the American artillery opened up with a frightening crash and started plastering the street down which the two soldiers had just disappeared. Savelsberg's heart leapt for joy. Perhaps the enemy shells had killed the artillerymen.

That night the old tram-driver decided to carry out a personal reconnaissance to find out whether the two soldiers were dead. As soon as it was dusk, he crawled carefully through the ruins, across an abandoned allotment, towards the cutting that went underneath the nearby railway line. Just as he reached it, the American guns opened up again. A furious bombardment descended on the city. Hastily Savelsberg ducked into the cutting. Six foot high and seven feet broad, it was the safest place around. Savelsberg was to spend the next seventy-two hours in that underground chamber, alone without a bite of food, while the world rocked and whirled crazily all around him, as if he were the last man alive in Aachen.*

But all was not sadness and fear in the strange underground world inhabited by Aachen's remaining civilians. Even the presence of the frontline, only two hundred yards away from No. 232 *Lennestrasse,* the 'last house in Aachen' as it became known later, could not dampen the spirits of the six Baurmann children, hiding in the house's cellars. The SA had ordered the family to join the evacuation, but one of the Baurmann children had whooping cough and was going to have to be left behind. Frau Baurmann had refused to abandon her child; instead she had 'gone underground' with her brood, a young aunt and her 72-year-old mother-in-law, Maria Kalff.

Grandma Kalff, a resolute, bold woman with snow-white hair, was the power in the Baurmann family. She kept the high-spirited children in order, organized food and water, and got rid of wandering soldiers, attracted to the house by the pretty young aunt and her 15-year-old niece Margit. Once a young infantry lieutenant wanted to set up his command post in the cellar, but Grandma Kalff had managed to get rid of him by telling him the air around the 'last house in Aachen' contained 'too much metal'. A sudden outburst of machine-gun fire convinced him that she was right. He beat a hasty retreat.

Then the soldiers of the 116th Panzer had taken the Baurmann brood under their wing. Whenever SA or SS patrols appeared, looking for civilians, they told them that the whole area had been evacuated days before. 'Who would want to live within two hundred yards of the *Ami* line?' they asked, and the SS and SA had believed them.

* He survived to tell his tale. The two soldiers had been killed after all.

Now, each morning, at the command of Grandma Kalff, known to the children behind her back as the 'High Command', Margit and her aunt Edith stole out into the morning mist to fetch water from a nearby well or potatoes from the surrounding fields. Soon the two city girls learned to milk too, drawing milk from the five or six cows left behind by the local farmers. Sometimes, whenever there was a break in the small arms fire, they were forced to leave their cellar and beat off wandering pigs, which broke into the orchard behind the house to forage for fallen pears.

Once one of the young soldiers stationed in the line facing the Americans brought them a freshly shot rabbit. That evening the Baurmann family invited the infantryman and his friend to dinner. When the rabbit had gone, greedily devoured by the children who hadn't seen meat for weeks, they were sent to bed.

The soldiers had brought schnapps with them. Under Grandma Kalff's eagle eye, the two young girls were allowed to have a glass. Later when the children were asleep, one of the soldiers disappeared to return with an ancient gramophone and a few records. Grandma Kalff gave her permission and the girls danced with the soldiers in the damp cellar. But at midnight 'the High Command' ordered no more dancing. So they settled down to listen to that sad, little song which symbolized 1944 for most Germans:

'Es geht alles voruber
Es geht alles vorbei
Nach jedem Dezember
Gibts wider ein Mai'*

* Everything passes, one day it'll all be over. After every December, there's always a May.

Next morning when the girls awoke, the two soldiers had gone as well as all their comrades in the line two hundred yards away. During the night the Germans had moved back nearly five hundred yards, in expectation of a new American offensive. Now the 'last house in Aachen' was well and truly in the centre of no-man's-land. Now there were no more young soldiers to bring them rabbit and gramophone records. Anxiously, even the children now subdued, the Baurmann family settled down to wait for the day when the first *Ami* tank would nose its way down the cobbled road towards Number 232 *Lennestrasse,* heralding the start of the new offensive.

CHAPTER EIGHT

By that third week of September, while the British 1st Airborne fought and bled at the bridge at Arnhem, Lightning Joe Collins planned his next attack on Aachen. After the failure of his 'reconnaissance in force', he realized that it would have to be a well-planned infantry attack, concentrating on the city itself with no attempt to by-pass it with armour, as he had originally intended Rose's Third Armored Division should do.

Now he planned, once the supplies were moving again and he had the air support he required, to launch his most experienced infantry division, the 'Big Red One', through the West Wall, east of Aachen in the vicinity of Eilendorf. From there they would seize Verlautenheide and push on to Wurselen, where they would link up with their comrades coming up from the other flank. Once the two groups had joined up, Aachen, so Collins reasoned, would be sealed off from the rest of Germany by a ring of steel. Thus, while the rest of the 1st Army pushed on towards its next major objective, the Roer River, the city itself could be reduced at the Americans' leisure. But before Huebner's 'Big Red One' could play its part in the great plan, his other infantry division, coming up from the west would first have to break through its section of the West Wall. In essence, everything depended upon the soldiers, who liked to call themselves 'Roosevelt's Butchers'.

'Roosevelt's Butchers', the name that the US 30th Infantry

Division had given itself, had first entered combat two years after the 'Big Red One', on 10 June, 1944. For several weeks its conduct, under the command of General Leland Hobbs, had been undistinguished. Then on the morning of 7 August, 1944, five panzer and SS divisions, the whole of Hitler's reserves in France, had struck the section of the Normandy front held by the 30th Infantry. It was the long-awaited German counter-attack, which Hitler hoped would throw the Allies back into the sea.

Unfortunately for Hitler, thanks to British Intelligence's 'Ultra'* system, General Bradley had already been able to warn Hobbs to expect a German attack. For five days and five nights, the 30th fought off the elite of the German Army at Mortain. It even produced a legendary 'Lost Battalion', comparable to the famous one of the First World War, which held out, completely cut off behind the enemy lines, standing up to everything the Germans threw at it. In the end the SS withdrew and started their long trek back to the Reich.

The 30th's reputation was made. General Bradley called the battle at Mortain 'one of the epochal struggles of the war'. Churchill named it 'one of the most daring'. And thereafter Bradley was proud to call the 30th the 'Rock of Mortain'. But the GIs, busy counting the piles of enemy dead heaped in front of their foxholes, were more direct in their choice of a nickname. They called themselves 'Roosevelt's Butchers'.

But by September, 1944, there were not many of the original 'Butchers' left. The six-week campaign across France, Belgium and Holland had taken its toll. Private Elmer S. McKay, a 19-year-old mortarman replacement, recalls arriv-

---

* See the author's *Battle for Twelveland* for further details of this secret organization.

ing in the 30th's lines during a bombing raid: 'There was a blinding explosion and I was tossed about like flotsam.' Recovering from this initial shock, he lined up with the rest of the replacements: 'I counted 33 men, which I thought was a rather large number of replacements for an infantry company whose total complement was 190 men plus five officers.' McKay was posted to E Company, 119th Regiment. While walking over to their lines, the German artillery suddenly opened up and the officer who had been in charge of the replacements, plus two of the new men, was killed instantly. McKay thought it 'peculiar that the wives or parents of those boys would be soon getting telegrams saying that their loved ones had been "killed in action". The poor things had never seen any "action".'

Little did the scared replacement realize it then, but by the time the battle for Aachen was over, he would be a platoon sergeant himself, the sole survivor of the men who had come with him, in charge of thirty men whose average age was just nineteen.

Officially, during that third week of September, the 30th Infantry Division was still resting. Just behind the line the Division had set up showers which were run like a Detroit assembly line. A filthy, ragged soldier from the line would go in at one end, where he would be ordered to strip, and emerge at the other clean, deloused and clad in a freshly laundered, if sometimes ill-fitting uniform.* Further back still there were a few rest centres, staffed by blue-uniformed Red Cross girls who served coffee and doughnuts all day

---

* Frontline soldiers, as the author can testify, would carefully examine these clean uniforms for darned holes which indicated a bullet wound. Uniforms of this kind were regarded as bad luck for the new wearer.

long, where battle-weary soldiers could chuckle over Bill Maudlin's caustic cartoons at the expense of the brass, or ogle the bold-eyed 'sweater-girl' pin-ups at the back of *Yank* magazine and listen to the brassy sound of Major Glenn Miller's 8th Air Force band being relayed from London.

Yet, in spite of the fact the Division was resting and the news agencies reported all was 'quiet on the Aachen front', there were still casualties. Many were from 'trench foot', caused by persistently wet feet; and behind the lines the dressing stations and field hospitals were full of soldiers whose toes had turned a dull purple. If they were lucky, the medics caught the complaint in time and they would be put to bed in long lines of cots on which lay soldier after soldier, their feet sticking out from under the blankets, with a little ball of cotton separating each toe. If they were unlucky their toes would come away with their wet socks when the medics had finally eased them off.

Some of the worst casualties were caused by the enemy snipers and on some sectors of the 30th Division's front, the riflemen only dared move in the early morning and after dusk. As one member of the Division's medical service recalled later, with much attention to clinical details:

'The sniper's finger presses the trigger and the bullet passes through the helmet, scalp, skull, small blood vessels' membrane into the soft sponginess of the brain substance in the occipital lobe of the cerebral hemisphere.

'Then you're either paralysed or you're blind or you can't smell anything or your memory is gone or you can't talk or you're bleeding—or you're dead.

'If a medic picks you up quickly enough, there's a surgeon who can pick up the bullet, tie up the blood vessels, cover up the hole in your head with a tantalum metal plate. Then, slowly, you learn things all over again, whether it's talking, walking or smelling.

'But if the bullet rips through your medulla region in the back of your head (about twice the size of your thumb) or if it tears through a big blood vessel in the brain—then you're dead, buddy!'

A couple of hundred yards away the German soldiers felt no happier. One such soldier, Lance-Corporal Herbert Gripan, sharing a foxhole with an older man, who slept most of the time when he wasn't on guard, felt cold and miserable, trying to keep warm with blankets taken from the bodies of dead comrades.

Occasionally the two men, for whom this was the first time in the frontline, talked about what they would do when the *Amis* captured them. The older man told Gripan that he had heard rumours that the *Amis* shot all prisoners they captured wearing the Iron Cross, first class.

But neither man really believed the rumour. They agreed that capture by the Americans was nothing to fear. Not that they intended to surrender. Indeed there was little talk of surrender, in spite of the seemingly hopeless position of Aachen. Naturally some of their comrades said it would be better to be captured and come home after the war with one's limbs intact. But no one dared talk openly about going over to the enemy, only two hundred yards away. After all, as Gripan told his comrade, they were 'fighting on holy German soil'.

Besides, for those of the defenders who had families back in the Reich, there was always Reichsführer Himmler's warning to the troops, widely publicized that September, that 'certain unreliable elements seem to believe that the war will be over for them as soon as they surrender to the enemy. On the contrary. It must be pointed out that every deserter will be prosecuted and will find his just punishment. Furthermore, his ignominious behaviour will entail the most severe consequences for his family. Upon examination of the circumstances [leading to the desertion] they will be summarily shot!'

Thus, if the hard-pressed defenders of Aachen were afraid of the coming American attack, they were even more afraid of the pale-faced, ex-chicken farmer, who had become the most feared man in Europe in the last five years.

In spite of the mood of many of his troops, General Koechling, who had replaced Schack at the head of the 81st Corps on 20 September, felt confident of his ability to defend the old Imperial city against the American attack. Now he had four divisions under his command, including Engel's 12th Infantry and the newly arrived 246th People's Grenadier Division, under Colonel Gerhard Wilck, which had relieved von Schwerin's 116th Panzer and in whose sector lay the city of Aachen itself.

Together these four understrength divisions numbered about 20,000 men. In addition, Koechling, a more aggressive commander than Schack, commanded 239 guns of various calibres, plus two assault gun brigades, and the 506th Tank Battalion and the 108th Tank Brigade, which numbered between them eleven tanks.

Yet, although his numbers were still small, when compared with the four divisions of 80,000 men that Collins could throw into the attack if necessary, General Koechling believed he could beat the Americans off when they came. He knew that he had Hitler's support; hadn't the Führer once prophesied that his Third Reich, like Charlemagne's First Reich, would last for 1,000 years?* To strike at Aa-

---

* Hitler regarded the Holy Roman Empire, which lasted until 1806, as the First Reich, Bismarck's Germany from 1871 to 1918 as the Second Reich, and his own as the Third Reich.

chen was, in effect, to strike at a symbol of National Socialist faith.

Thus, when Field-Marshal von Rundstedt promised him that he would receive a reformed 116th Panzer and the 3rd Panzer Grenadier Division in the first week of October, a total of 24,000 men, Koechling believed the ancient military genius, who had now taken seriously to the bottle on account of the machinations of the man he called contemptuously 'the Bohemian Corporal';* for Hitler himself was behind the move.

So, as September gave way to a grey, wet October, General Koechling, although not complacent, was confident he could throw the *Amis* back when they came.

By now General Leland Hobbs had put the final touches to his plan to penetrate the West Wall. His 'Butchers' were dug in along the River Wurm between Geilenkirchen and Kerkrade. From their foxholes on the left bank of the river, they could already see the outline of the bunker line against which they were to launch the first set attack.

Their Commander's plan was simple. His infantry would pierce the line of bunkers. As soon as that objective was achieved, the attached tanks from the 2nd Armored Division would cross the Wurm and swing eastwards to seize the crossings of the Roer River, only nine miles away. His 'Butchers', on the other hand, would strike east of Aachen itself and drive towards Wurselen.

In order to achieve complete success, Hobbs had decided to limit the front of his attack to exactly one mile, stretching between the villages of Rimburg and Marienberg. His reasoning was simple. Although the site was far away from the 'Big Red One', which would launch its attack on the other

* Hitler had been a corporal in the First World War.

side of Aachen, it would not involve his men in street fighting. This way his Division would not get bogged down in costly, time-consuming house-to-house combat.

To increase his chances of getting across the Wurm and through the first line of fortified defences swiftly, he had enlisted the support of the 9th TAC Air Force. Already his artillery observers had pin-pointed 75% of the pillboxes along the mile-length stretch of front through which he would attack. Once his men did start to cross the river, a rolling artillery barrage would precede them, while 360 bombers and 72 fighters and dive-bombers would blast the pin-pointed bunkers and all the rearline German supply roads and tracks. They would be followed thirty minutes later by fresh planes carrying America's newest secret weapon—the terrifying napalm bomb, to be used that October for the very first time.

In the meantime the assault infantry were already preparing to cross the River Wurm, which patrols had discovered was not so deep as it had been drawn on US military maps, by a novel means. Each rifleman would carry with him into the attack a section of wood, which he would toss into the river as soon as he reached it. In this way, it was hoped, the total amount of wood thrown in would suffice to get them across with, at the most, wet feet. As soon as they were through and had formed a bridgehead, then the combat engineers would begin preparing proper bridges for the follow-up troops.

Thus, as the supplies of ammunition, bridging equipment, gas and oil started to mount up in great dumps behind the 30th's lines and the planners worked feverishly, night and day, to ensure that nothing could go wrong on the day of the attack, 2 October, 1944, General Hobbs was as confident as his opposite number General Koechling that he would triumph. His 'Butchers', keyed-up and tense, were no less confident. As they began to receive extra rations of chocolate and cigarettes prior to the attack, they joked easily among themselves about 'fattening pigs for the kill'.

Back at First Army HQ, Verviers, General Hodges was optimistic too, something quite unusual in that slow, plodding cautious General. On 28 September, with three days to go, he even ventured to send his boss, General Bradley, a present which exemplified his optimism. It was a handsome bronze bust of Adolf Hitler with the following inscription at its base:

'Found in Nazi Headquarters, Eupen, Germany.* With seven units of fire and one additional division, First US Army will deliver the original in thirty days.'

That proud boast would never be realized. Due to Koechling's stubborn defence of Aachen, preventing Hodges's First from advancing any deeper into the Reich, Hitler was to be granted enough time to raise a great new army and plan a major offensive from the Eifel below the Imperial City. It took another nine months before Hitler was finally vanquished. And before then, the US Army would fight its greatest battle of the war in Europe—the Battle of the Bulge—at a cost of 80,000 casualties.†

But as that wet September week neared its end, with a heady confidence reigning everywhere on the Allied side of the front, no one would have even considered the possibility

* Eupen was actually in Belgium, although it had been incorporated into the Reich in 1940.

† Hitler had dreamed up his original plan for the 'Bulge' on 16 September, the very day that Collins' 'reconnaissance in force' had finally ground to a halt at Aachen.

that Hodges's proud boast would be proved so badly wrong
and that Hodges himself, the commander of half a million
men, would one day be fleeing from his own HQ, with the
Tigers of the Adolf Hitler Bodyguard Division hard at his
heels.

BOOK TWO:
THE HARD SLOG

'If the 116th Panzer and the Adolf Hitler are in there, this is one of the decisive battles of the war.' *Corps Commander General Corlett to General Hobbs, 12 October, 1944*

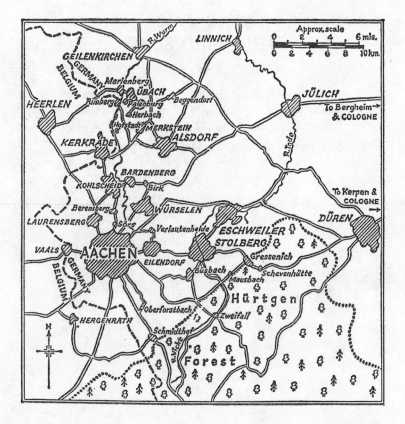

CHAPTER ONE

MONDAY, 2 October, 1944, dawned dull and overcast. From outside his command post, General Leland Hobbs watched the grey sky to the west anxiously. Soon the 300-odd medium bombers would be coming in from England to strike the West Wall defences, and the General was worried about the safety of his own forward troops. It wasn't the first time the US Army Air Corps had bombed the 30th Infantry Division; he hoped it wouldn't happen again. At precisely nine o'clock, as planned, they came winging their way in. Three hundred odd of them flying low over the battlefield at 250 mph. Here and there the German flak opened up. Black cottonwool puffs of smoke flecked the grey, leaden sky. Still the two-engined Mitchells came on. The General and his staff focused their binoculars. They saw the bomb-doors in the planes' bellies open. A moment later the bombs began to tumble in haphazard profusion from the Mitchell's silver bellies.

Then General Hobbs groaned out loud in horror and anger. The bombs were falling wide of their target! Bomber after bomber missed. Not one bomb struck the pillboxes of the West Wall. The whole air strike, which Hobbs regarded as essential for the success of his attack across the Wurm, had been useless!

There was worse to come. A little later Hobbs heard from a member of his staff that one group of bombers had missed not only the target, but the country as well. Instead of releasing their bombs over Germany, they had dropped them over Belgium! Mistaking the Albert Canal for the River Wurm, they had bombed the nearby Belgian mining village of Genk, almost destroying it and causing 79 casualties, including 34 dead.*

As ten o'clock came and the last of the Mitchells roared off to the west, back to England, the tense expectant infantry crouching in their damp foxholes on the other side of the Wurm knew the air attack had been a total failure. The pillboxes across the river were still intact.

As one private soldier recalled later: 'We had heard stories about the thousands of planes that were supposed to have come and destroyed the pillboxes, but we only saw a few of them and the damage was slight.' It was a finding confirmed by one of the 30th's first prisoners, who remarked when asked what he thought of the effect of the American bombing, 'What bombing?'

'The American Luftwaffe', as the GIs of the 30th Infantry were now calling the 9th TAC Air Force, which had carried out the raid in part, was living up to its reputation for making a mess of things.† But in spite of the failure of the raid, Hobbs knew the infantry attack must go on. The order went out: 'Prepare to attack!'

With a tremendous roar, 400 American guns and mortars opened fire on the one-mile long front. A few seconds later the frontline machine guns joined in, cutting lines of tracer through the smoke of exploding shells. But again the watching, waiting infantry could see that the artillery bombard-

* One of the village's most celebrated inhabitants at that time was the Polish emigrant Edward Gierek, a 31-year-old miner, one day to be the Communist head of Poland.

† During the Battle of the Bulge the 9th's reputation sank to an absolute zero when it bombed the town of Malmédy, held by the 30th, and killing a large number of GIs and Belgian civilians.

ment was not living up to Hobbs's expectations. As one infantryman recalled: 'The 6omm mortar shells bounced off their pillboxes like peanuts, but at least they caused the personnel inside to duck.' But not all of them ducked. Immediately after the initial shock had worn off, the German defenders opened up with counterfire. Within a matter of minutes, the Germans had destroyed five of the eight machine guns in action on the 1st Battalion's front.

The whistles began to blow. The heavily-laden riflemen started to stumble out of their holes. Carrying the wooden boards, they doubled down the muddy western slope of the Wurm's valley, through the soggy, shell-pitted fields, ridged with beets and turnips, and on to the river.

Lieutenant Don Borton grabbed his board, waded waist-deep into the cold water with the enemy slugs hissing across it all around him, and flung it into place. 'There's your goddam bridge!' he yelled to his hesitant men. 'Come on!' They hesitated no longer. They, too, began flinging their boards into the river. Minutes later they were across and on the other bank eleven Germans popped up out of their holes and started yelling frantically, '*Kamerad, Kamerad, nicht schiessen!*'

But not all of the initial wave were so lucky. To Borton's right, another company of riflemen were caught by a sudden concentration of German shells. Within minutes 93 of them had been killed and wounded out of a total of 120. That was the end of that particular company's attack on the Wurm.

Fresh troops were flung in. Now the Americans were scrambling across the River Wurm everywhere. But once the troops had crossed the river, many of them were flinging themselves down behind the cover of a railway embankment on the far side. The sight annoyed 1st Lieutenant Robert Cushman, who, ten minutes before, had received a telegram from the States announcing that his wife had just given birth to a baby boy. Standing out there in the open, with the slugs cutting the air like a shower of tropical rain, he yelled at his men to advance. A little later Cushman fell wounded, one of the ever-increasing number of casualties.

Inspired by his leadership, Private Youenes crawled to within ten yards of the nearest German pillbox. On his back he carried the infantry's deadliest weapon—a flame-thrower. Crouching on the concrete structure's blind side, he pressed the trigger. Bright scarlet flame tinged with black oil embraced the bunker. An instant later the concrete charred a deep black. The flame-thrower spat again. From within came the sound of muffled screams.

Youenes doubled forward and thrust an explosive charge attached to the end of a long pole through the nearest aperture. There was a thick crump. Black smoke poured from the hole. Seconds later the five German survivors, their uniforms in tatters, their faces black, their limbs trembling, came staggering out to surrender.

The 'Butchers' had no time to rest on their laurels, however. They pushed on. Again Youenes went into action. But this time the German garrison of the pillbox did not surrender without a fight. A bare-headed German officer rushed out, brandishing his pistol. He fired wildly at the advancing infantry. A rifleman dropped dead.

In an instant, over a dozen men had turned their weapons on the German officer. He crumpled up, his body riddled with bullets. Thereupon the six men remaining alive in the bunker surrendered.

And so the slaughter went on. Both sides suffered severe casualties, as the 'Butchers' fought from pillbox to pillbox, forcing the Germans steadily back towards the little village of Palenburg. A flame-thrower operator fell dead, the bullets striking his container, so that his body was wreathed in a funeral pyre an instant later. His comrades used a bazooka in its place, blasting great holes with the rockets in the pillboxes and inserting hand grenades into the holes to force the defenders to surrender.

By four o'clock that first afternoon, the leading infantry were fighting in Palenberg itself, forcing their way from house to house against stiff enemy resistance. Now the battle had become a series of grim hand-grenade duels between individual German and American soldiers, crouching in the smoking ruins of the village.

One infantryman, Private Harold Kiner, spotted a German stick grenade as it landed between him and two mates. Immediately he flung himself upon it. His back arched as it exploded beneath him. But his action saved his two friends. Later he was awarded America's highest award for bravery, the Medal of Honor. But by then he was long dead.

But if the Americans were successful at Palenberg, they were facing serious trouble by the evening at the village of Rimburg, in the shape of the moated, onion-towered baroque *Schloss*. Just as the American attackers approached the castle, they bumped into a large German bunker, expertly camouflaged as a house. It stopped them dead with its concentrated machine-gun fire.

Hastily the infantry called for assistance from their 'big friends'. But the Shermans of General Harmon's 2nd Armored Division, the elite 'Hell on Wheels', which had been whipped into shape after its formation in 1940 by General George Patton himself, had not yet been able to get through the deep black mud on the other side of the Wurm. They could not reach the trapped infantry.

Desperately Colonel Sutherland, in charge of the assault

regiment, threw in another battalion. They crossed the
Wurm on a bridge made of doors and fence posts. They
pushed through the demoralized survivors of the original attack. Intense small arms fire met them from the walls of the
castle. Suddenly it seemed as if they were back in the eighteenth century, as rifles opened up from slits in the walls and
from the shattered windows. Still the troops pushed on, taking heavy casualties as they advanced through the debris-littered park, its ornamental baroque figures pock-marked
with bullets. By nightfall they had succeeded in forcing the
Germans from the castle walls and moat and had built up a
defensive position on three sides of the castle. But inside the
defenders, protected by the three-foot thick masonry, still
held out.

Unknown to the Americans, the castle, which belonged to
a cousin of the head of the German Army at the outbreak of
the Second World War, Field-Marshal von Brauchitsch, was
connected to a bunker two hundred yards away by an underground tunnel, through which new men and fresh supplies of ammunition could be brought to the hard-pressed
defenders.

Meanwhile, as the battle began to die away for that day,
the Americans started to collect the dead. It was a tragic
sight, as one of the Dutchmen, a resident of the village of
Rimburg, who had helped to guide the Americans to the attack, remembered thirty years later: 'I was exactly thirty
then, but all my sixty years, I never saw anything so terrible.
That morning I'd seen them go into the attack—strong,
young men. That had been from a distance. Now I saw
them at close hand—*dead!* It was awful. Everywhere there
were helmets, pieces of human bodies, torn uniforms. I was
so sickened that I couldn't get a bite of food down that
night.'

The dead were loaded into jeeps, covered with sheets of canvas, and driven away into the darkness.

On the morrow the Americans attacked again. This time Harmon managed to get his tanks into action. His plan called for his Combat Command B to swing north through and behind the West Wall to where the Thirtieth Division was fighting to blast all hell out of the defenders in their pillboxes.

But it was not to be as easy as the General had anticipated. As he recalls in his memoirs *Combat Commander*: 'The Germans put up a ferocious resistance . . . The elimination of the pillboxes was slow and dangerous work. Some we disposed of by firing tank shells or 155mm rifled artillery through their gun slits. Others, held by particularly determined defenders, fought on until tank-dozers [armoured bull-dozers] heaped up earth around their rear doors and buried the occupants alive!'

Indeed his progress was so slow at one point, where the commander in charge explained his lack of success by the fact he had run into 'a murderous crossfire from dug-in anti-tank guns and artillery', that General Harmon was forced to relieve the officer and replace him by a more aggressive commander.

By now Rimburg Castle had fallen and the captors were already drunk in its great cellars, swilling the choice Rhenish wines they had found there. Further on, Rimburg village itself was afire. The Germans were already beginning to withdraw under the pressure of the advancing Americans. The bridge went up, with it a large store of potatoes kept near by. Seed potatoes showered the advancing infantry. But they did not find the matter very funny. They were taking too many casualties.

The first GI peered into the cellar at No. 13 *Dorpstraat*,

which housed Netta Schurer, a Dutch woman and her four children, plus a mixed bag of Germans and Dutch people, sheltering from the battle at the castle only four hundred yards away. He saw Netta trying to clean the lice from her youngest child's head, the result of spending the night among the lousy straw which covered the floor. He backed out hastily. Up above in the burning street, another Dutchman, Frans Allon, stopped an advancing American jeep, containing three soldiers. '*Niet verder . . . niet verder!*' he screamed at them frantically in Dutch. 'No further . . . the Germans have mined the road ahead!' Somehow the GIs understood. Shouting their thanks, they swung the jeep around and tore back the way they had come.

Frits Eygelshoven, the 20-year-old son of Rimburg's chemist, was not so lucky with his warning that day. Warned by his friend Frans Hermans that the Germans had left a large dump of shells behind, near a farm which could explode at any moment, he decided to tell the Americans. Braving the bombardment the two Dutch boys ran down the street. A shell landed on a nearby farm. They ducked and ran on, leaving behind them the groans of the wounded. Another shell landed nearby. Suddenly Frans Hermans found himself flying through the air, as if transported by some huge, invisible hand. He was slammed against a broken door and fell to his knees. For what seemed a long time, he remained there. Then he shook his head and rose to his feet. Where was Frits? Three yards away Frits Eygelshoven was lying on the cobbles, unconscious, blood pouring from a wound in his forehead, his left arm ripped off!

Today, three decades later, 50-year-old Frits Eygelshoven recalls that it 'took me ten years to find myself again. It was hard,' and he looks reflectively out of his kitchen window at the restored Rimburg Castle only three hundred yards away.

That same afternoon, as the fighting started to die away, General Harmon himself drove up to have a look at Rimburg Castle. To him, 'its interior seemed to be from a story book; marvellous tapestries hanging from the walls and splendid carved wooden furniture and magnificent silverware gave mute testimony to the good life someone had once lived there.' Harmon's orderly suggested that he should install one of the electric warmers they had found in one of the bathrooms in his own caravan. Harmon refused. He was very strict on the matter of looting, both with his men and himself.

But his strictness was to no avail. Later that day when he re-passed the Castle, he 'saw a number of trucks belonging to rear echelon and Air Corps units parked outside the castle. The vehicles were piled high with the baron's possessions.' Harmon went on his way, reflecting on the scandalous behaviour of the 'canteen commandos', the rearline troops. As he was to write about the episode long afterwards: 'Very little of such pillaging was done by combat troops; their discipline was higher, they had no way to transport booty, and perhaps most important, they were too busy fighting to have time to steal other people's property.'

But now the fighting had begun to die away in the bridgehead, as the October gloom grew thicker. The weary troops, who had been fighting since early that Tuesday morning, slumped down in the smoking ruins or on the muddy fields and grabbed an opportunity to eat one of the issue chocolate bars, known cynically among them as 'Hitler's secret weapon' on account of its effect on their digestive systems. On the other side of the line the German 'stubble-hoppers', who were equally weary, dug ravenously into cold cans of 'Old Man', the standard *Wehrmacht* meat ration, reputedly made up of dead, old men, their haggard, unshaven faces starkly silhouetted against the flickering light of the still burning village of Rimburg.

The River Wurm had been forced successfully. At the cost of some three hundred dead and wounded, 'Roosevelt's Butchers' had gained a very narrow bridgehead along the whole mile of front, as planned by their commander. Although their bridgehead was not particularly spectacular, Hobbs was pleased with himself that evening as he ate his usual hearty meal at his headquarters; the Division now had a foothold on enemy territory from which it could launch its attack towards Wurselen.

But at the same time the General was a little worried. As he turned in later that night to the sound of his own guns, the ever-present background music to war, one question was uppermost in his mind. What would his opposite number *General der Infanterie* Koechling do, once he had recovered from the shock induced by the new American offensive?

CHAPTER TWO

THE answer was nothing. The night hours passed leadenly and still the Germans, feared by the Allies for the speed with which they usually launched their counter-attacks, did not come. Back at his HQ, Koechling himself was surprised and angered by the fact that General Lange, commanding the 46th Division, facing the Americans on the Wurm front, had still not moved. The local infantry commanders explained that they could not attack on account of the 'murderous enemy artillery fire'. In the end Koechling insisted. But the counter-attack was a half-hearted affair, consisting of a handful of infantry and two assault guns. It was beaten off by the 30th Division easily with the Germans retiring after an hour, leaving seven dead behind them. They didn't come again that night.

Now it was the Americans' turn once more. At dawn Hobbs sent other elements of his Division in the direction of the village of Uebach. Their mission was to cut the main Geilenkirchen-Aachen road and occupy the high ground east of the road between Uebach and Beggendorf.

But the American assault force, supported by Harmon's tanks, soon ran into serious trouble. Entering the village of Uebach, they found the place full of fresh and determined troops. The Shermans retired hastily. Too easy a target for the German infantry armed with the feared *panzerfaust*, they scuttled for safety, leaving the village to the infantry. Bitter house-to-house fighting developed up and down the battle-littered cobbled streets. A door kicked open. In with the grenade. A frightening crump. A rapid burst of sub-machine-gun fire and the mad, scared rush inside, guns blazing to finish off the dazed survivors. Over and over again, with the attackers steadily getting fewer as the day progressed. And still the village would not surrender.

Next day the fighting continued and little quarter was given or expected. Two successive commanders of the lead battalion were killed within an hour of each other before finally, at four o'clock, the last house in the ruined village was taken and the Americans could begin to advance again. For over two hours after they had moved out, the boxlike Red Cross ambulances with the ominous sign in the windshields 'Carrying Casualties' were kept busy evacuating the dead.

The 30th Division pushed on to Hoverdorf and Beggendorf. In the latter village Sergeant Ezra Cook found a telephone intact in a captured bunker. He did not hesitate. Whirling the 'phone's handle, he called to the next German-held bunker and commanded in an odd mixture of German and English: 'We've just taken your comrades. Now we're coming to take you.'

The threat worked. Moments later twenty-five German soldiers came streaming out, their hands held high in the air.

The advance continued. By the morning of 5 October, the 'Butchers' had reached a line stretching from Beggendorf, through Uebach and on to Herbach (still in German hands) and from there to Hofstadt, held by both Americans and Germans.

Back at his Command Post, General Hobbs was pleased with the progress his Division had made. Over the last three days his advance had cost him nearly 1,800 of his 'Butchers'. But still the price had not been too high. He had broken through the West Wall in the first set-piece attack on the fortifications and soon his men would be in a position to threaten the key objectives of Merkstein, Boesweiler and Alsdorf. If General Koechling did not act soon, it could be a matter of a day—two at the most—before the 30th was in a position to link up with the 'Big Red One', which was scheduled to begin its own drive on 8 October.

But on that Thursday *General der Infanterie* Koechling had received a surprise visitor at his CP, who had steeled his resolve considerably. It was no less a person than the Minister of Propaganda himself, the limping, little 'poisonous dwarf' (as his enemies called him behind his back), Josef Goebbels. And the Minister of Propaganda, a Rhinelander himself, who had dedicated National Socialist Germany to all-out war the year before with his rallying cry of *'Wollt Ihr den totalen Krieg?'* * was not the man to allow Koechling to forget his duty as a 'loyal National Socialist officer'. That night his firm order went out to General Lange, commander of the German 49th Infantry Division: 'Attack and drive the Americans back across the Wurm!'

That same day there was one lone pillbox not yet occupied by 'Roosevelt's Butchers' in the fortified line east of the village of Herbach, which was still in German hands. During the afternoon Lieutenant Parker, commanding the leading platoon of infantry, had argued that it shouldn't be left in the enemy's possession. But the commander of the supporting tanks from the 2nd Armored had stated that he had not enough ammunition left to attack it; he would leave the capture of the pillbox to the following day. It was a fatal oversight, for it was that particular bunker which General

---

* 'Do you want total war?' His demand to the assembled German workers and soldiers at his speech at the Berlin *Sportpalast*, 1943, which signalled a turning-point in the war for Germany.

Lange decided to use as a forward base for his new counter-attack against the *Amis*.

At dawn, two battalions of his infantry were in position on both sides of the bunker, ready for the attack. As the first watery rays of the sun broke the morning mist, two Mark IV tanks hidden behind the bunker itself clattered into the open and started firing at Parker's dug-in infantry. Moments later three other tanks appeared and added their fire to the others. Parker's men, surprised and frightened, lost their nerve. Instead of sticking it out in their foxholes, they broke and ran for the cover of the bunkers they had taken the day before, forgetting the lessons they had learned during the last few days. Once inside they were trapped, as had been their previous German occupants.

The German infantry seized the opportunity. Though lacking the American flame-throwers, they pinned them down with small arms fire and assaulted the entrances with hand-grenades. In rapid succession they took one pillbox after another, taking over a hundred American prisoners, including three officers. Frantically the American regimental commander, Colonel Cox called for tank support. But Harmon's Sherman crews suddenly discovered they needed urgent maintenance and scuttled off to the rear; it would be a long and bloody two hours before someone or other forced them to return to the scene of the fighting.

The Americans went on to the defensive. Dug in around the two pillboxes left in their hands, the GIs, supported by heavy American artillery fire, stuck it out grimly and held up the 49th Division's advance.

Then it was the Germans' turn to make a bad mistake. Just as the two infantry battalions were about to launch their last attack against American defenders of the trench line, their covering artillery lifted its fire a few minutes too early, before they had closed with the *Amis*.

The 'Butchers' grabbed the opportunity offered them with both hands. Springing from their foxholes, they poured a murderous hail of fire into the advancing Germans. The enemy soldiers fell by the dozen, great holes torn in their ranks at such close range.

It was just at that moment that the first of another group of Shermans appeared. Under the command of Lieutenant Walter Macht, the Sherman, whose 75mm gun could get off six rounds for every one of the hand-operated German Mark IV, knocked out three enemy tanks in quick succession. That was enough for the remaining two. Abandoning the infantry to their fate, they swung round and clattered hurriedly to the rear and safety.

The men of the 49th started to follow suit. Here and there officers, armed with Schmeisser machine pistols, tried to rally them. But it was no use. The volume of American fire was too heavy and the Shermans were joining in with the co-axial machine guns. They broke and ran, leaving their wounded behind them. The 'Butchers' followed at close range. One by one they recaptured the pillboxes they had lost that morning. General Koechling's second counter-attack had failed miserably.

Enraged by the lack of success of his ground troops, Koechling ordered his Corps artillery to pour all the fire it could muster onto the advancing Americans. The handful of Luftwaffe fighter-bombers at his disposal were also commanded to join in the attack. All that afternoon the 81st hammered the narrow bridgehead with all they had, with no regard to their rapidly diminishing supply of ammunition.

For many of the shell-shocked Americans, cowering at the bottom of their muddy trenches it was the heaviest barrage they had experienced since the attack at Mortain in the previous August. As one man recalls: 'It was really big stuff. It came in like an express train!'

Young Pfc Elmer McKay, the newest recruit to the 119th Infantry, was caught by it in Bardenberg. As he remembered later: 'Together with my new friend, Alfred Berlan [killed near Jülich in February, 1945] we were so tired we didn't care what happened and we found ourselves in the cemetery beside the big church at Bardenberg. We stretched out one blanket on the pebble path and both sat down on it; we took the other blanket [each soldier carried one blanket] and covering our feet first we then brought it up over our bodies to the neck and laid down. Immediately a 20mm gun opened fire . . . the shells coming down the cemetery path . . . missing our noses by what must have been inches! We rolled away from each other out of the path and ran like scared rabbits. The German gunner must have sat and watched us doing all this not really wanting to kill us, but once we found ourselves comfortable he had remembered his duty and fired to let us know he was there.'

Pfc Elmer McKay had lived to fight another day. But many of his comrades in the 30th Division didn't, as the Luftwaffe fighter-bombers zoomed in over Palenburg, in groups of twenty and thirty, an unprecedented number for that period of the war, to release their bombs.

But neither the artillery barrage or the aerial bombardments particularly impressed a visitor to Koechling's HQ that afternoon. Field-Marshal Model, the monocled, gross-looking officer, who had won his reputation as the 'Führer's Fireman' in Russia because he could be sent to any part of the front where there was trouble and be guaranteed to put out the blaze, wanted something more than that.

But the reserves promised to Koechling by Field-Marshal

Rundstedt had not made their appearance. And Germany's most energetic and effective commander, who in less than eight months' time would shoot himself because he knew the Russians had labelled him a 'war criminal'* had to stand by, fuming and impotent, as the Americans prepared to attack again. Now the 81st Corps had no reserves left. The barrel had been scraped clean!

The seventh of October became a day of exploitation for the Americans. Led by tanks, the 'Roosevelt Butchers' charged two miles along the road leading into Alsdorf. The attack was a walkover. Once the initial resistance had been broken, the German front seemed to crumble away. 'Alsdorf was a ghost town,' one American officer remembers. 'It was so damned quiet that it scared you.'

The American tanks pushed on. A heavy German anti-tank gun tried to bar their way. A score of cannon were trained on it. It disappeared in an instant. Two German officers, unaware that the Americans had already broken through, bumped into the column in their staff car. The leading Sherman opened fire. The German car burst into flames at once. The two officers were burnt alive. The column rolled on.

By midday they had reached Reichsstrasse 57, Aachen-Monchengladbach, and had taken it. Now the beleaguered city could be reached by one main highway from outside; Reichsstrasse I, Aachen-Jülich–Dusseldorf. Aachen was virtually cut off!

The infantry advanced into the grim coal-mining town of Merkstein. After the Allied fighter-bombers had softened it up, they started to move towards the German defensive line. The Germans began firing back. Most of the riflemen

* Today, Model's body, rescued from its secret wartime grave, rests in a military cemetery, not twenty miles from Aachen.

ducked and sought cover. But a single, dark-skinned Pfc, Salvatore Pepe, began a little private war of his own. Firing his M1 continuously and throwing grenade after grenade, he wounded four of the German defenders and 'persuaded' fifty-three more to surrender. The action won him a medal for bravery and contributed greatly to the surrender of the town.

Now the German front was crumbling everywhere and the exuberant commander of the US XIX Corps responsible for this part of the front, General Corlett, reported to Hodges: 'We have a hole in this thing big enough to drive two divisions through!'

General Hobbs supported Corlett: 'I entertain no doubts,' he said, 'that this line is cracked wide open.'

And General Hobbs was right. Now the West Wall bridgehead was six miles long and four and a half miles deep. Thus he could now report to his Corps Commander: 'The job is finished as far as this division is concerned,' and added a special plea that he hoped the First Army Commander would appreciate 'what this division has done'.

Happy and confident that Friday night, General Leland Hobbs, probably assuming that he had a good chance of taking over the corps that would be soon vacant, would never have dreamed that before the month of October was out Hodges would be considering him not for promotion but for demotion in disgrace!

But at that moment General Hobbs felt that he and his 'Butchers' could rest on their laurels for a while. His division had done what had been asked of them. Now it was up to General Huebner's 1st Infantry Division. The 'Big Red One' could carry the ball the rest of the way.

CHAPTER THREE

'THE trouble with the "Big Red One",' soldiers in other divisions were wont to say, 'is that it thinks the US Army consists of the First Division and ten million replacements.'

The 'Big Red One' had good reason to think itself superior to the rest of the Army. At 0605 hours on 23 October, 1917, its artillery had fired the first shot by American troops in Europe in the whole history of the United States Army. Thereafter it was the first US Division to meet the enemy in battle, the first to suffer casualties, the first to stage a major offensive, the first to enter Germany. In the Second World War it was the first American formation to reach England; the first ashore in the invasion of North Africa, Sicily, and Normandy and the first to crack the West Wall. (It might also be pointed out that, following both wars, it was the *last* division to return home to the States.)

With its slogan of 'No Mission Too Difficult, No Sacrifice Too Great, Duty First', the 'Big Red One' was a world of its own; its men proud, arrogant and cocksure. Indeed, after its first year of action, General Bradley was forced to relieve the then commanding general, Terry Allen, and his deputy, General Roosevelt, because 'Under Allen the 1st Division had become increasingly temperamental, disdainful of both regulations and senior commands. It thought itself exempted from the need for discipline by virtue of its months on the line.'

In Allen's place, Bradley appointed Major-General Clarence R. Huebner, who enlisted in the Army as a private in 1910 and had fought with the 'Big Red One' as a captain in the First World War. (At the Battle of Soissons in 1918, he was the only officer left standing in the whole of the 26th Infantry's 2nd Battalion.) Thereafter Huebner had worked his way steadily up the ladder, gaining himself a reputation during the process of being a flinty disciplinarian, who set great store by spit and polish.

Thus, when he took over the 'Big Red One' in Sicily in 1943, his first measure was to set up a rigid drill and training programme; and his veterans didn't like it one bit. As General Bradley records in his memoirs: 'Christ,' they exclaimed in disgust, 'here they send us a stateside Johnny to teach us how to march through the hills when we've been killing Krauts! How stupid can this son-of-a-bitch get!'

Right from the start General Huebner was determined to show the 1st US Infantry Division that he was boss, and he didn't care how strong the men's animosity towards him was. Thus, when in the last week of September General Collins ordered him to carry out his part in the sealing off of Aachen, he did not hesitate, although his Division was holding more than twelve miles of front along a semi-circle west, south and east of the city. (The manual prescribed *six* miles of front for a division against first class troops like the Germans.) His only concern was where he would be able to free enough men from his overlong line to launch the attack.

In essence, his infantry had the objective of capturing Verlautenheide and pressing on to Hill 239, to which his troops had given the ominous name of Crucifix Hill because of the great wooden cross which surmounted it, and from thence to their final target Hill 231 (Ravelsberg). On the face of it it was not a mammoth undertaking. The distance to be covered was only two and a half miles. But those two and a half miles were packed with German pillboxes, enjoying excellent fields of fire. And that was not General Huebner's only worry. If and when his infantry managed to capture their three objectives, they would be badly exposed on a thin salient, open to enemy attack on both sides.

In the end Huebner decided he would protect one side of that salient, once he had linked up with Hobbs's men coming from the other flank, by launching an attack into the city of Aachen itself. He had thus given himself four objectives.

Satisfied with his plan, Huebner ordered his men to step up their training—this after four months of combat in Europe!—for the great attack, which had been going on for a week now. Under the command of Colonel Smith, who would lead the attack, they started to apply the lessons they had learned in their first encounter with the West Wall in September. Special pillbox squads were set up. Equipped with flame-throwers, satchel charges and Bangalore torpedoes, they would attack the enemy pillboxes on the hills in front of them under the cover of 155mm mobile guns firing at pointblank range. To support them, Colonel Smith would have at his disposal, eleven artillery battalions, plus air support if the weather improved.

But Colonel Smith, knowing General Huebner's bad temper and intolerance of failure, was taking no chances. He convinced the other two regimental commanders that they should launch a feint attack to distract the Germans. And to make absolutely sure of success, he decided not to attack at dawn as was customary with American commanders. He would attempt to catch the Germans off guard by attacking under the cover of darkness.

Thus the veterans of North Africa, Sicily, Normandy and Belgium trained and waited. Their days were spent in the sodden, dripping fields to the west of Aachen under leaden skies; their nights in their shell-pocked, battle-scarred billets, listening to Glenn Miller on BBC, London, chewing on tasteless rations, leafing through old copies of *Stars and Stripes*.

As one of them recalled that period of waiting: 'You sweat out your turn for a hot shower and you stand in it as long as you can. You want to stay in it for hours and you rub yourself with soap again and again, trying to get the stink out of your body and the mud out of your mind and the war out of your soul—for a few minutes anyway.

'Then you climb back into your dirty smelly clothes and go back to your muddy foxhole where the war is.'

Thus the 'Big Red One' trained and waited.

On 7 October, the same day that General Hobbs stated that 'I entertain no doubts that this line is cracked wide open', General Huebner announced the date of his attack—one hour before dawn on Sunday, 8 October, 1944.

Verlautenheide was taken in a rush. The German defenders, caught off guard by the night attack and cowed by the sudden, massive bombardment, cringed at the bottoms of their foxholes and were taken prisoner almost before they knew what was happening.

Led by Captain Bobbie Brown, a company of infantry rushed Crucifix Hill, the 'Big Red One's' first objective, under artillery cover. The great wooden crucifix which dominated the hill was struck. With a harsh, rending sound it started to fall, as if God himself had given up on this terrible world of men gone crazy.

Captain Brown and his infantry had no time for symbols. From their bunkers, the Germans opened a frantic fire on the advancing Americans. Brown was wounded and wounded again. And then a third time. Still he did not waver. He pressed home his attack, personally knocking out three of the pillboxes.

The end came suddenly. Everywhere the Germans started waving white flags, raising their arms and yelling 'Kamerad'. Crucifix Hill was American.

The next night, objective number two fell to the 'Big Red One'. Slipping in two companies of infantry past silent enemy bunkers, Colonel Smith captured the Ravelsberg (Hill 231) without a shot. Unaware that the vital height had been taken, the German rear echelon sent up four men with the next day's supply of food for the 65-man garrison. To the cooks' consternation, they were received not by their comrades but by the tired, mud-stained and very hungry Americans. In spite of the fact the ration containers were filled with what the German soldier called 'giddiup goulash', a stew reputedly made of horsemeat, the GIs did credit to it.

So, within forty-eight hours, the 'Big Red One' had captured its two primary objectives. General Huebner was highly satisfied. He knew he could expect German counter-attacks soon, but he felt confident he could ward them off. Now it would only be a matter of a day or so before General Hobbs's 30th Division linked up with him and the ring around Aachen closed.

It was a view supported by Field-Marshal Model himself. He reported to Rundstedt that 'the situation around Aachen grows more critical'. Unless the promised reinforcements arrive very soon, 'continued reverses will be unavoidable'.

Now, on the night of the 9th, General Huebner decided it was time to deliver his ultimatum to the Battle Commandant of Aachen: either the Germans surrendered or they accepted the terrible consequences.

At ten o'clock on the morning of 10 October, while the guns fell silent all along the 'Big Red One's' front, three lonely American soldiers began their solemn march down the middle of Aachen's shattered Trierer Strasse. Silently, knowing that enemy eyes were watching them from the ruins on both sides of the long street, they turned down the Adalbertsteinweg and at Aachen's main square, now the heart of the city's defences, the Kaiserplatz, went right.

In the centre of the strange little trio was Pfc Ken Kading, bearing a big white flag over his shoulder. On his right marched 1st Lieutenant William Boehme from New York, whose parents had emigrated to the States from Germany. He spoke fluent German; he would be the interpreter. On Kading's left was 1st Lieutenant Cedric Lafley who would do the negotiating.

As the three soldiers marched towards the Command Post of Colonel Leyherr, the city's Battle Commandant, the civilians watching from their cellars already knew why they were there. For days now the *Amis* had been shooting shellloads of surrender leaflets into the city, and the propaganda of nearby Radio Luxembourg, by now in American hands, guided by the expert knowledge of Staff-Sergeant Hans Habe,* had already warned them of the dire consequences of not accepting the American terms.

After the formal preliminaries, Lafley handed Leyherr General Huebner's ultimatum and asked him to read it. It read (in part): 'The city of Aachen is now completely surrounded by American forces . . . If the city is not promptly and completely surrendered unconditionally, the American Army and Air Force will proceed ruthlessly with air and artillery bombardment to reduce it to submission.

* Today a popular German writer and, although a Jew, the advocate of a strict nationalist course.

'In short, there is no other way out. Either you surrender the city . . . or you face total destruction. The choice and responsibility are with you. Your answer must be delivered to the spot designated by the bearer of this document within twenty-four hours.'

Leyherr did not hesitate. He knew well enough what happened to any German officer who incurred the Führer's wrath. He rejected the ultimatum out of hand. Let the *Amis* do their worst. The Battle for Aachen would continue.

The next twenty-four hours passed in tense expectation. Leyherr refused to receive a delegation of local citizens who wanted to attempt to make him change his mind. All he did was to tell them that the population could be accommodated in a group of bomb-proof bunkers, if necessary. That night the 'Greater German Radio' announced proudly that Leyherr had rejected the American offer 'coldly and out of hand', while the US press proclaimed *'Assault on Aachen is on!'* They were not mistaken.

At 12 o'clock on 11 October, American artillery began pinpointing selected targets in the city with red smoke-markers—the goods station, the university area, the Lousberg height, etc.—prior to the air attack. Minutes later the American Lightnings and Mustangs zoomed in at 300 mph. Below them Aachen lay wide open, defended only by a handful of anti-aircraft guns. Time and time again they roared in in groups of six and seven, dropping their five-hundred-pound bombs with deadly accuracy. Sixty-two tons within a matter of sixty minutes.

At the same time twelve battalions of artillery poured their fire onto the centre of Aachen. Just short of 5,000 shells were fired, weighing 169 tons. Within minutes the city centre had disappeared in a thick cloud of smoke.

The first wave of dive-bombers disappeared. Liesel and

her sister Kaethe Krehwinkel ventured out to hang up their washing and begin baking a loaf of bread in the oven they had made in their garden. But they didn't get far. In the distance they could already see the next wave of *Ami* bombers homing in on their target. They fled, leaving the washing strewn over the debris-littered garden. Once again they pelted down the steps to the cellar in which they had already spent three weeks. They were to spend another three in it before they saw daylight again.

Dusk began to fall. Still the bombardment of the city continued. In Cologne the evening edition of the National Socialist paper *Westdeutscher Beobachter* proclaimed proudly: 'In a thousand years' time our heirs will speak of the great battle for Aachen and the example it gave to the people in the west of the Reich during the terrible battle.'

But in the ruins all that the frightened civilians were conscious of was the booming American loudspeakers of the Psychological Warfare companies announcing that if the city did not surrender by the next day, the bombers would come again.

CHAPTER FOUR

MEANWHILE the battle to close the gap between the two infantry divisions—the 30th and 1st—continued. But it was running into trouble. On the First's front, the strain was beginning to tell. A soldier, laying a chain of anti-tank mines on the Ravelsberg, carelessly caused one of them to explode. Before anyone could act, the mine set off a chain reaction. When it was over, thirty-three men lay dead, dying and wounded. A company commander, leading a relief company towards his own position, was fired on by a trigger-happy sentry. He yelled that he was from the 'Big Red One'. More of the trigger-happy defenders joined in and before someone finally realized that they were firing on their own men, most of the relief company had been wounded or killed outright. Suddenly General Huebner began to run out of men to put into the line.

Hobbs, who had been so confident three days before, no longer felt so optimistic about his chances of closing the gap either. By now he had lost three thousand riflemen, about one third of the division's effectives, and his men were running into ever increasing trouble. On the same day that the Air Force had begun its massed attacks on Aachen, his men, who had taken the village of Bardenberg with hardly any opposition, suddenly found themselves trapped by a battalion of the 108th Panzer Brigade, which had infiltrated the village with tanks and half-tracks.

Desperate house-to-house fighting developed. Major

Howard Greer, the local battalion commander, went out personally hunting tanks. He knocked out two with his bazooka before he was forced to take cover. Sergeant Pendleton, although wounded, drew the fire of the enemy machine guns upon himself so that his squad could advance down one of the narrow village streets. He was killed in the process. American fighter-bombers entered the fight, zooming in at roof-top height to knock out the German vehicles. Tank after tank went up in flames. But still the battle raged.

Pfc McKay recalls that 'the fields to the right of the road were literally covered with American dead . . . I lay there under heavy shellfire and a shell landed within a metre or two of me . . . there were three of us lying side by side and I was closest to the explosion. The force of the shell lifted me into the air and I fell back shaken but unwounded. The boy in the middle was wounded badly by shell fragments which miraculously missed me. The boy farthest from the explosion was immediately killed.'

By nightfall Bardenberg was back in American hands, with six German tanks and sixteen half-tracks knocked out. The road to North Würselen was opened again. But now Hobbs, like Huebner, was running out of reserves, and intelligence was reporting disturbing rumours—the reformed 116th Panzer, von Schwerin's old division, had been spotted back in Aachen!

General Hobbs's fears were justified—and more. Not only had the 116th arrived back on the Aachen, but also the 3rd Panzer Division, promised to Koechling by Field-Marshal Rundstedt. And that wasn't all. Already Hitler had begun to assemble a new secret SS panzer army for the last great offensive in the West, later to be called the 'Battle of the Bulge'. One of the units belonging to that secret force—the 6th SS Panzer Army—was the elite 1st SS Panzer Division, the Adolf Hitler Bodyguard. Now the Führer ordered that part of that force, the 1st SS Battalion, Battalion Rink, named after its commander, be detached to aid the beleaguered garrison in Aachen.

Rink's men were in an ugly mood. A few days before they had been called out to clear up after an American air raid on the nearby town of Düren, and what they had seen there—'women literally smeared against the walls of houses by the bombs'—made them ready to 'castrate the Americans who did that with the edge of a broken bottle!'

The SS men attacked immediately. They flung the Americans out of North Würselen and forced them back beyond the West Wall, but at a terrible cost. Just before Rink started to move his command into the city of Aachen itself he ordered a count of his men. His NCOs reported that out of the 274 other ranks and 32 NCOs who had gone into action the day before, only 142 other ranks and 25 NCOs were left. In just over 24 hours, the Battalion had lost nearly 50% of its strength!

Just after dawn on 12 October, the Germans counter-attacked all along the 30th Division's front. A three-hour fight started at the village of Birk. Sergeant Melvin Bieber, commanding the only American tank stationed at the crossroads inside the village, knocked out one German tank and forced another to flee. But still the Germans did not give up. Five more enemy Mark IVs emerged out of the mist. At the last moment, when Bieber thought he was going to be overrun, fresh Shermans from the 2nd Armored arrived. One after another the Mark IVs were blasted to a halt. Yet the enemy panzer grenadiers continued their attack, now without the support of armour. They knocked out every one of the infantry's guns. The 'Butchers' fought back violently. By ten-thirty the fight was still in progress and the American commander, harassed but proud of his command, reported to General Hobbs by radio, 'I never did see men going like these have been going . . . we are as strong as we can be.'

At Würselen Captain James Burt of the 2nd Armored saw a group of 'Butchers' run straight into a murderous hail of small arms fire, followed by a barrage of six-barrelled electric mortars. Captain Burt did not hesitate. Springing down from the turret of his Sherman, he ran towards a rise beyond the infantry. Immediately the enemy switched their fire. Standing there fully exposed, Burt directed his Shermans into a position from which he could defend the pinned-down infantry. Subjected to almost pointblank enemy fire, he was wounded in the face and then again in the neck. But he had saved the 'Butchers'.*

Attacked on the road to Würselen, Pfc McKay ducked into the hallway of a nearby house. The Battalion's artillery observer snapped at him to get further inside; in the doorway he was a perfect target for the enemy snipers. The artillery observer followed, but paused in the hallway to take a last look outside. At that moment an enemy sniper fired. The artillery observer sank to his knees, shot through the chest.

Shortly afterwards the enemy counter-attack broke off for a while. McKay ran with some of his mates to the aid of one of the machine-gunners slumped over his glowing gun. To their surprise they found the man wasn't dead. 'In fact, he acted as though he had just awoke from a deep sleep . . . he had run out of digitalis for his heart, something none of us knew he had been taking and which should surely have

---

* In spite of his wounds, Burt continued to fight for another eight days and for so doing won the 2nd Armored's only Medal of Honor of the Second World War.

precluded him from front-line duty. Further investigation showed *that he also had a glass eye!*[*]

McKay's surprises were not yet over for that day. Just before sunset, with the battle still raging, 'we looked across the fields and saw somebody running in a peculiar manner, as though wounded or ill. It was obviously not a soldier. As the person came closer, we realized it was a pregnant woman, wounded in the leg. We took her back to a *Bierstube* on the road where that night she gave birth to a baby boy, delivered by Dr Phillip Ferrier, our battalion surgeon.' In the midst of death, new life!

The news of the enemy counter-attacks shocked Hobbs and Corlett. As Corlett said to Hobbs: 'If the 116th Panzer and the Adolf Hitler (1st SS) are in there, this is one of the decisive battles of the war!'

At the headquarters of the 'Butchers', the staff began to talk in hushed tones of a 'new Mortain', where the Division had gained its nickname.

By noon Hobbs was on the defensive everywhere and was glad to report to his superiors that 'the Germans are nibbling and pushing, but (so far) no general attack'. Everything, he felt, was fairly under control.

General Hodges was not so sanguine. He was not content just to hold the enemy counter-attack; he wanted action. His Army had spent too much time and lost too many men already at Aachen. He wanted to get on with his drive to the Rhine. Angrily he told General Corlett, 'We have to close that gap. It will have to be done somehow!'

But as that second week of October passed, with Hobbs's men stalled everywhere, the gap between the 30th and the

[*] After that, according to McKay, 'he was taken from the front lines and we never saw him again.'

1st Divisions remained obstinately opened. Now both Corlett and Hobbs began to fear for their posts. Later both of them confessed that they felt they were 'walking on eggs' with Hodges. The Army Commander's impatience grew. 'Hobbs,' he observed to his staff, is always 'either bragging or complaining.' Privately he told Corlett, 'I always thought you ought to relieve Leland. He hasn't moved an inch in four days!'

In despair the Commander of the 30th Division appealed to Corlett for support. But the Corps Commander, who had already seen the writing on the wall, met his every appeal with the same harsh command: *I want that gap closed!*

CHAPTER FIVE

On the same morning of 12 October, 1944, that American Secretary of State for Defense, Henry L. Stimson was telling the press in Washington that 'No German city is taboo for us. The Nazis will have to choose between surrender and destruction. Otherwise there will be twelve other "Aachens" on German soil',* Colonel Leyherr was relieved of his post. Leaving at the 'personal command of the Führer', he was to die in action in the spring of 1945 for a cause in which he no longer believed.

The man who replaced him was Colonel Gerhard Wilck, who had been in the German Army since 1916. His career had not been brilliant. At the outbreak of the war he was still a major and it took another year before he was promoted to lieutenant-colonel in Norway, where for three years he commanded an occupation regiment spread over six hundred miles. In 1943 he was sent to Russia, where he promptly landed in one of the many 'pockets' of that year of disaster. Fortunately for him, he was one of the 4,000 men out of 60,000 who managed to escape from the Russian trap. One year later he was promoted to full colonel and given command of the 8,000-man strong 246 People's Grenadier Division, made up of ex-sailors, ex-Luftwaffe air crew without planes and a few new recruits, all of them without infantry training. It was with this untrained division that Wilck

* He had been asked whether he would be prepared to have Aachen destroyed if it didn't surrender.

arrived at the Aachen front on 25 September where he promptly protested to Field-Marshal Model that the 'sack of Aachen' could not be defended: the main defensive line should be moved beyond the city. Model flushed crimson and bellowed at him, 'The Führer has commanded that we will not give up one inch of ground. His command is holy for us!' And that had been that.

By the second week of October most of Wilck's untrained ex-pilots and submariners had been killed by the advancing Americans. Eager but untrained as they were, his Division had been easy meat for the enemy. Wilck was a commander with virtually no command. Thus it was not surprising when his old acquaintance, the 7th Army Commander General Brandenberger, picked him to replace Leyherr as Battle Commandant of 'Fortress Aachen', though the Army Commander had tears in his eyes when he handed Wilck the formal declaration that he would not surrender to sign. Hitler now insisted that all his fortress commanders should sign such a document. Brandenberger felt he was sending his old comrade to his death. For the Colonel, who had served with him in the same regiment twenty years before, had now sworn on oath not to surrender Aachen; if he did, then Hitler was empowered by the document he had signed to seize his family and have them executed. And Wilck loved his family; he would rather risk death than surrender his wife and children to the Gestapo.

So on the night of 12–13 October, 1944, Colonel Wilck set out on his dangerous journey from Brandenberger's HQ at Munstereifel to his new command in Aachen. His mood was grim. As a former tactics teacher, he knew that Aachen was a hard place to defend. It was surrounded on all sides by hills; the enemy would be virtually looking down his throat all the time. Of course, the advantage in the house-to-house fighting to come would be on his side, providing the troops under his command were of better quality than his decimated People's Grenadiers. But he knew, too, that the American domination of the heights and the air would mean his own men would only be able to move at night. During daylight hours the environs of Aachen would belong to the Americans.

But as the single staff car, containing his batman, Corporal Karl Schulz from Hamburg, and the newly appointed National Socialist Leadership Officer [a kind of Nazi political commissar], approached the beleaguered city, Wilck dismissed his gloomy thoughts. First things first, he told himself. For a start he had to concern himself with getting into the city. But that task proved surprisingly easy. Some civilians showed the driver a ford across the River Wurm. Without the slightest difficulty their Opel drove through the river, which was already in American hands, and on to Aachen.

An hour later Colonel Wilck was bent over the large-scale map of Aachen at his HQ in the Hotel Quellenhof, studying the situation of his new command with the aid of a flickering candle. It was not too good. To the north-east the 1st American Division had firmly established themselves. To the west the position was the same and now the Americans were slowly gaining control of Würselen. It was obvious what their intention was. They wanted to link up and cut off his last remaining axis of supply—Reichsstrasse 57.

Wilck ordered one of his staff officers to give him a quick rundown of the forces available. They consisted of nine different units, made up of some 2,000 men of varying quality, ranging from the survivors of his own untrained division to the elite parachute tank-hunting company and the men of the 1st SS. To support them they had several batteries of artillery, including the city's former flak cannon, and a handful of tanks, assault guns and armoured personnel carriers from the 341 and 217 Assault Gun brigades. It wasn't much to stop a three-division enemy attack, but Wilck, mindful all the time that the life of his family depended on his actions, set about organizing the defence of the city as best he could.

He ordered a rifle battalion to be rushed to defend the vital Reichsstrasse 57. The remaining 88mm cannon of what was left of his own 246th People's Grenadier Division were emplaced, at his command, on the high plateau to the north-west of the city to shell any American advance from the direction of Würselen. Then he formed a battle group from the best troops under his command, Rink's SS men, and the remaining armour of the two assault gun brigades. They would form a ring around his own command post and make up a last-ditch defence if the Americans succeeded in breaking through towards the centre of Aachen.

Satisfied that he had done all he could do for the present, Colonel Wilck slumped back in his chair and waited for the dawn. As the first light started to flush the sky over the silhouette of the ruined city towards the east, he received his first message as Battle Commandant from General Brandenberger. It read: 'Hold out. Large-scale help on its way.'

It was dawn on Friday the 13th.

Nothing happened. That Friday both sides in the month-old battle for Aachen seemed like punchdrunk boxers, still in the ring but swaying with exhaustion, apparently too worn out to level the final punch, kept on their feet by sheer nervous energy. They had reached a stalemate.

Back at his HQ General Hobbs, an old school commander who had not much faith in manoeuvre, realized at last that his head-on attack on Würselen was not paying dividends. After fighting for four days since crossing the River Wurm and establishing his initial bridgehead he had advanced exactly one thousand yards! Something new had to be tried. That Friday he came to the conclusion that two routes offered a way out of the impasse: he could drive south along the east bank of the River Wurm and strike south along its west bank. In this manner he might be able to outflank the enemy. In spite of earlier objections to these manoeuvres by his staff that they would involve both a river crossing and frontal attack against pillboxes, still held by the Germans, Hobbs decided he would try both. It seemed to be the last chance open to him of breaking the deadlock on the 30th Division front and avoiding the necessity of a showdown with Hodges, who was now obviously out for his blood.

His plan, therefore, was this. Two battalions of infantry under Colonel Sutherland would cross the Wurm into the village of Kohlschied before dawn on the 16th. They would head south along the west bank of the river. Another battalion would then cross the Aachen–Würselen–Linnich highway north-west of the Ravelsberg. And, as he warned Colonel Sutherland at the initial briefing that day, there would be no half measures this time. This time it would be 'root-hog or die!'

Thus it was that a surprised and pleased Colonel Wilck enjoyed two days of grace, which he quickly used to his advantage. That night a long convoy of trucks crept down the sole open road, bringing with it supplies for the trapped garrison. Twenty-five tons of ammunition were pumped into the garrison's depleted reserves. More important, Rink's SS men used the cover of darkness to break off a small local action with the Americans which had been holding them up all day and reach the centre of Aachen, ready for Colonel Wilck's orders. Aachen, which Wilck had thought that morning, might well fall within a matter of hours once the Americans attacked in strength, would live to fight for another two weeks.

But already the brass was celebrating the fall of Aachen. As Friday gave way to Saturday, General Hodges, with his HQ in tents pitched in a muddy field outside the Belgian chateau of Ensival on the edge of the town of Verviers (he was the only senior commander still under canvas), waited expectantly for his illustrious guests who would be coming from Luxembourg, France and Belgium that day. No less a person than King George VI had invited them to a celebration dinner.

Eisenhower arrived first, from Verdun. He made a detour to have a look at the Aachen front personally. As Kay Summersby records: '[There] he got a first-hand view of the ruins of Aachen—and a first-hand view of the mud when he slipped and fell flat on his face in the mire to the cheers and laughter of the hundreds of gleeful troops!'

But the General was not the only one to have an unusual experience that day. Along with the American General Hart, his escorting officer, the King had enjoyed several cups of tea at Field-Marshal Montgomery's HQ that morning. Thereafter the King and the American General had been rattling over the rutted Belgian roads towards Verviers for several hours until General Hart could stand it no longer. He murmured, red-faced and embarrassed, to the King that he had to stop the convoy for a 'sanitary halt'. The King was puzzled. But his mystification was soon solved when he saw what the 'sanitary halt' entailed. As the convoy started again, he turned to his aide, smiling: 'Be sure to include that in the diary.'

The King was in high good humour at the lunch held in

the chateau's barren dining-room into which Hodges had moved grudgingly for the occasion. Surrounded by the American brass, ranging from Eisenhower and Bradley down to Hodges' corps commanders, Collins and Gerow, he listened to General Patton, as the 3rd Army Commander related his experiences during the North African campaign. He spoke of the Tunisian Arabs' long fingers and their habit of stealing even from the wounded, adding to the King: 'Why I must have shot a dozen Arabs myself!'

Eisenhower looked at Patton and winked at Bradley: 'How many did you say, George?' he asked.

'Well, maybe it was only half a dozen.'

'*How many?*' Eisenhower persisted.

Patton laughed and, turning to the King, said, 'Well, at any rate, Sir, I did boot two of them squarely in the,—ah, street at Gafsa!'

Thus the brass celebrated the 'completed encirclement of the roofless city of Aachen', as General Bradley phrased it proudly, little aware just how premature their celebration was. For General Huebner's 'Big Red One' was barely hanging on to what it had gained, its soldiers daring only to leave their foxholes at night on account of the snipers who seemed to be everywhere; while General Hobbs's 'Butchers' were bogged down completely, with their commander afraid that if he didn't pull something out of the hat very soon, he would be relieved. And the gap between the two divisions was still not closed.

CHAPTER SIX

AT 0500 hours on the morning of 16 October, Colonel Sutherland's infantry began to cross the River Wurm. Luck seemed finally to be favouring 'Roosevelt's Butchers' once again. Opposition was light. Within half an hour, the lead battalion had reached the outskirts of Kohlscheid and everything seemed to be proceeding according to plan.

But Hobbs's main effort, allotted to the 2nd Battalion, 116th Infantry Regiment, didn't run so smoothly. They had just attacked the enemy pillbox line when they were counter-attacked by SS men of the new SS Battlegroup formed by Wilck two days before. The force of the German attack was so strong that the riflemen were compelled to go to ground when only half-way to their primary objective, Hill 194.

Sergeant Holycross of the 2nd Battalion, who had already shown during the 30th's initial attack on the West Wall nearly a month before that he was something of an expert in reducing pillboxes, belied his name yet once again. Slipping round the German flank, persuading some of the pinned-down infantry and a couple of Shermans to follow him, he set out to break the SS resistance. Ordering the tanks to pin down the SS troopers with the 75s, he crawled through the pouring rain with a handful of infantry to begin his assault on the first pillbox. It fell as did the next one—and the next. In the end the sergeant captured or destroyed seven pillboxes and took fifty SS men prisoner. The advance could go on once again.

But not for long. As the American commanders tried to push their infantry through the gap cleared by Sergeant Holycross, German artillery, sited on a neighbouring hill, opened up. The air was suddenly torn apart by the howl of enemy mortars and ripping sound of the 100-lb shells hurled by the German 88s. The infantry went to ground once more, while Sherman after Sherman of 2nd Armored ground to a helpless stop in the thick mud.

But Hobbs's luck had not run out altogether this miserable Monday morning. Just at that moment a diversionary attack went in to the east. Immediately the SS men turned their attention to meet what they thought was a new threat. The German artillery bombardment began to slacken. The trapped American infantry needed no urging to get moving again. Leaving their dead lying in the mud-churned fields, they pushed forward once more.

Meanwhile, another American diversion began to help the main attack. Under the command of Captain George Sibbald, a company of infantry thrust forward south-east of Alsdorf towards the positions held by the grenadiers of the 116th Panzer Division, located astride a slagheap and a railway embankment. But, to the advancing riflemen's surprise, they met very little resistance, although the enemy positions were excellent. They advanced more swiftly. They had just passed the entrance to the Gouley Mine when screaming panzer grenadiers started to emerge from holes in the ground *behind* them. They had walked into a cleverly designed trap.

For an hour and a half, Captain Sibbald fought desperately to extricate his men. But in the end he had to order the withdrawal of the riflemen who had not been caught in the enemy trap—fifty out of a company of 130 men. He had lost over 50% of his strength.

But, in spite of the losses incurred by the companies carrying out the various feints, the troops executing the main push were advancing on their objective slowly but surely, with the pressure on them being lifted by an alarmed German command, which felt it was being attacked now on the whole length of the American 30th Division's front.

The afternoon hours passed, with the Americans edging ever closer to their objective, while General Hobbs waited expectantly for news. Then at 1544 hours, as the wet October afternoon drew to its close, the chief-of-staff of the 'Big Red One' telephoned Hobbs. Excitedly he informed the Commanding General that 1st Division men posted on the top of the Ravelsberg had spotted American troops moving cautiously along the south-western fringe of Würselen. 'Roosevelt's Butchers' had finally reached their objective, Hill 194.

The 'Big Red One' was separated from the 'Roosevelt's Butchers' by exactly one thousand yards. The gap was almost closed at last!

But there was still some heavy fighting to be done before that one-thousand-yard-wide gap was finally closed. Newly promoted Sergeant Elmer McKay, already in charge of a mortar platoon after less than three weeks in the line, due to the many casualties suffered by the 30th Division, had just reprimanded one of his men for wearing a woman's fur hat instead of his steel helmet.

'Well,' the GI had replied, 'you always tell us to wear something on our heads to protect us, sarge, and I've lost my helmet—when the platoon hit a minefield. The lead man went down with his foot off.'

'It's no use trying with the detectors,' someone cried, 'they're S-mines.'

The young men's faces paled. They all knew that the wooden mines would not be detected by the engineers' electrically-operated mine detectors. One of their buddies was out there groaning in agony, his foot blown off.

In the end one of McKay's 'men'—the average age of the platoon was 19—volunteered to go into the field to try to get the wounded man out. Cautiously he started to probe his way into the field, feeling his way with the bayonet inch by inch. Behind him the rest of the platoon held their breath. Then they gave a collective sigh of relief. The young volunteer had made it!

The volunteer decided to make one last check before attempting to lift the man. Carefully he slid his bayonet into the damp earth just level with the man's shoulder—and hit a S-mine. There was a tremendous roar. Mud and gravel shot high into the air. Black smoke billowed upwards. When it cleared, the horrified spectators could see that the wounded man was dead and the man who had attempted to rescue him was severely wounded himself. The advance of Sergeant Elmer McKay's mortar squad came to an abrupt halt.

Up in the gap, the Germans were battling desperately to prevent the Americans linking up and cutting them off from the rest of the Reich. That day Lieutenant Zillies of the 116th's Panzer Grenadier Regiment won the Knight's Cross for his stubborn defence of his bunker: one of seven such awards gained by the defenders of Aachen during the battle.

Not far away the bunkers held by Lieutenants Mueller, Reisch and another unnamed young officer changed hands for the *sixth* time that day, and even when the Americans did finally link up, the three officers would still hold out for a further three days.

It was Sergeant Frank Karwell, of the 30th Division, who finally volunteered to take a patrol from the Division's advanced position on Hill 194 to make the link-up with the men of the 'Big Red One' awaiting them on the Ravelsberg. At first their progress met no opposition. Cautiously they edged their way across the churned-up fields, littered with American and German dead, getting ever closer to the objective which had occupied the attentions of a whole American Army for nearly a month now. Still the Germans did not spot them. The first 'Big Red One' foxhole line was clearly visible now, in spite of the pouring rain.

Then the patrol's luck ran out. Just as they were about to dash across the Aachen–Würselen road, a lone Spandau machine gun opened up. Sergeant Karwell yelped with pain and dropped to the ground. The rest of the patrol flopped down. They had been spotted!

While one of their number, crouched in a ditch, tried to bandage the Sergeant's wounds as best he could, sprinkling them liberally with sulpha powder, the rest of the leaderless patrol conferred on what to do next. All the time the lone German machine gun kept up its hammering, waiting for them to move.

In the end the patrol, trapped in the middle of no-man's-land, decided to stay where they were. There were two exceptions, the two scouts, Privates Edward Krauss and Evan Whitis. They said they were going to go on. Leaving the rest to their fate, they doubled across the road with the German bullets chipping the stone all around them and ran towards the Ravelsberg. Gasping with the effort, they started to climb the hill. Suddenly they came to a halt. Men in American uniforms were popping up from the foxholes dug everywhere above them.

'We're from K Company,' the men in the holes shouted joyfully.

'Come on up!'

'And we're from Company F,' Whitis and Krauss yelled back proudly.

'Come on *down!*'

But the veterans of America's oldest and premier infantry division talked faster and more persuasively. Krauss and Whitis sighed and continued their climb upwards to the waiting GIs of the 'Big Red One'.

It was 1615, Monday, 16 October, 1944. Finally the gap had been closed. The fate of the Holy City of Aachen was almost sealed now.

BOOK THREE:
THE LAST ROUND

'All ammo gone after severe house-to-house fighting. No water and no food. Enemy close to command post of the last defenders of the Imperial City. Radio prepared for destruction.' *Colonel Gerhard Wilck to HQ 246th People's Grenadier Division, 21 October 1944*

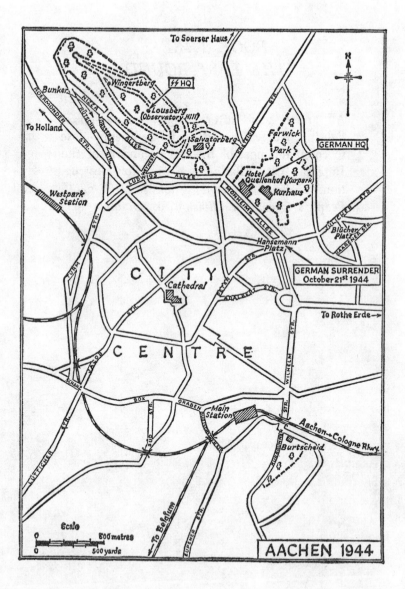

To Soerser Haus

N

Wingertberg

⚡⚡ HQ

Bunker

Lousberg
(Observatory Hill)

To Holland

Salvatorberg

Ferwick
Park

GERMAN HQ

Westpark
Station

Hotel
Quellenhof (Kurpark)

Kurhaus

Hansemann
Platz

Blücher
Platz

CITY

Cathedral

GERMAN SURRENDER
October 21st 1944

To Rothe Erde →

CENTRE

Main
Station

Aachen→Cologne Rlwy.

Burtscheid

To Belgium

Scale

500 metres

500 yards

AACHEN 1944

CHAPTER ONE

THE news that the gap had been closed went round the world, for it signified that the first German city to be attacked by the Allies would soon fall into their hands. In Luxembourg the military government teams, which would govern the city once it had fallen, were alerted to move. Aachen's military government would be the pilot scheme for the whole of occupied Germany. Closer at hand the press corps attached to the 1st US Army prepared to go into the city, as soon as the American press officers gave the word, eager to interview the Germans on their home ground for the first time. Everywhere there was a mood of new optimism in the Allied camp that the way to the Rhine was opened at last. Might not the imminent fall of the old Imperial City herald the collapse of the whole decrepit structure of the Third Reich? Back at Eisenhower's new Versailles HQ, Montgomery, cheerful in spite of his defeat at Arnhem, made a five pound bet with the Supreme Commander that the war would be over by Christmas. But the 17 October copy of the Army newspaper *Stars and Stripes* which blazoned the banner headline that the '*1st Closes Aachen Gap. 3 Assaults Smashed by Hodges*' on its front page, depicted a Sherman a little further down, firing into some ruins with the caption '*Siege of Aachen*'.

They were ominous words for those Americans in the know. Already that month the US Army had suffered 10,000 casualties taking the French coastal port of Brest, which

General Bradley was to admit was only 'a prestige objective', fought for solely on account of the 'honor of the US Army'.* But Aachen was not a prestige objective. It *had* to be taken if the Americans were to advance securely to the Rhine, whatever the cost.

It was a problem already seriously occupying General Huebner, whose division had been given the task of capturing the city itself. For two days now his infantry had been attempting to drive into the rubble-filled streets of the ruined city and they had not been doing too well. For a start he had only two battalions of Colonel Seitz's 26th Infantry Regiment to spare for the task and they were numerically inferior to the 2,000 odd men at Colonel Wilck's disposal, supported by thirty guns and five tanks. As he told Colonel Seitz, he must hoard his precious reserves for the German counter-attack against the link-up point between the 30th and 1st Divisions, which surely must come. Thus, Seitz was destined to avoid the battle for the ruined city, but at the cost of very high casualties. The 26th Infantry would have to attack, as one of Seitz's staff officers put it later, 'with one eye cocked over its right shoulder in the direction of the possible German counter-attack'.

As a result Colonel Seitz had been obliged to plan an attack on the city which would allow him to concentrate his two battalions, and not involve him in that dread of any infantry commander—house-to-house combat in a built up area. In essence, he had planned that his 2nd Battalion, under the command of Colonel Daniel, would attack along the Aachen–Cologne railway line at the Rothe Erde railway

* Due to the excessive casualties suffered at Brest, the US Command ordered that remaining coastal forts, such as Dunkirk, Lorient, etc., should be sealed off. So they remained, 500 miles behind the Allied lines right up to the end of the war.

station and then drive through the heart of Aachen towards the west.

Meanwhile his 3rd Battalion, commanded by Colonel Corley, would move from a position between Rothe Erde and Haaren, and move westwards to capture the three hills which dominated Aachen to the north—Lousberg (the Americans called it 'Observatory Hill' after the observation tower which dominated its crest), the Salvatorberg and the Wingertberg. From these three positions they hoped to be able to take the whole city under fire and in particular, the Hotel Quellenhof, which they knew from Intelligence was the headquarters of the city's new Battle Commandant.

That had been the plan and it had run into trouble right from the start. Colonel Daniel, who had been assigned the task of attacking along a 2,000 yard front right into the heart of the city, no mean undertaking, had given some thought to the assignment. He had decided to divide his 2nd Battalion into small squads, each accompanied by a tank or tank destroyer. Each squad would assault a carefully designated strongpoint under the cover of the tank's gun. Once the strongpoint had been captured, the tank would turn its attention to the next one and so on. For Colonel Daniel had assumed—correctly—that the Germans would defend every house and every cellar.

To ensure that contact was maintained between these little squads, the methodical Colonel had set up a series of checkpoints based on street corners and more prominent buildings. So that the enemy would not be able to slip in between two different squads and take them by the flank, Colonel Daniel had ordered that no squad would advance beyond a designated checkpoint before it had established firm contact with its neighbouring squad. Thus with every possible eventuality seemingly taken care of and demolition and flame-thrower teams standing by, just in case the softening-up tank fire did not prove sufficient, Colonel Daniel's men had moved into the attack.

Within a matter of hours the Colonel had learned that his plan had not covered every possibility after all. Just as a couple of his leading squads had cleared one of the first littered streets and were advancing to their next objective, confident that they had crushed all enemy resistance, dirt-smeared, grey figures had begun to emerge from the sewers in the street behind them.

The advancing GIs swung round in alarm. Too late! The Germans opened up with their machine pistols. Man after man dropped in agony. Within a matter of minutes, twenty or more of the 2nd Battalion's men lay on the cobbles, shot in the back. And before their startled comrades could react, their attackers had disappeared the way they had come, scuttling into the cover of the sewers.

On that day, the same scene had been repeated all along the 2nd's line of advance so that in the end Colonel Daniel had been forced to halt his men while another measure was put into force. From now onwards, all cellars had to be cleared before the infantry moved any further. In addition, each manhole and sewer cover had to be located in advance and blocked or sealed off when it was reached by the squads. Even before it had got underway, Colonel Daniel's drive had slowed down to a hard, frustrating slog.

Colonel Corley's men, driving towards the Lousberg, had not found the going any easier. By noon on the first day they had found themselves pinned down at the Blücherplatz. There a hail of fire had poured into the cautiously advancing Shermans from the direction of the German strongpoints at the St Elisabeth Hospital and the Technical College. A quadruple 20mm flak cannon, used in a ground rôle, joined in, sending a stream of shells straight down the Jülichstrasse at pointblank range. The riflemen of the 3rd Battalion had gone to ground immediately, scrambling for cover in the piles of rubble.

But there was no room to manoeuvre for the two lead Shermans. One was knocked out at once. The other was struck a moment later. In an instant it began to burn, throwing up a dense cloud of smoke. Sergeant Alvin Wise, a K Company squad leader sprang on to the Sherman's turret. He grabbed the turret machine gun and started spraying his front with bursts of tracer, although well aware that the tank could explode beneath him at any moment. His bold action inspired two other riflemen of his own company. Under the cover of the Sergeant's machine-gun fire, which prevented the enemy taking accurate aim, they too pelted towards the tank and clambered inside, pushing the wounded tankers out of the way. Although neither of them had ever even seen the inside of a Sherman before, they somehow started its motors, swung it round and drove it to safety behind the American positions.

But in spite of that minor triumph Colonel Corley, back at his CP, knew that his advance along the Jülichstrasse had bogged down badly at the Blücherplatz crossroads.

The same afternoon a Czech war correspondent, attached to the 1st US Army, was returning to Brussels to file his despatch to the Czech exile papers in London on what he had seen within the city in the last three days! 'I have seen the city of the German Emperors being wiped out after it had refused the offer of honourable surrender and I found its people crushed to desperation by a double misery, by our onslaught and by the cruelty of their Nazi masters. When I first approached Aachen, the town was burning. From an

American observation post, just above the city, I could see immense columns of smoke rising to the sky where some 60 Allied dive-bombers were freely forming up for attack and diving unmolested on to their objective. As the bombs came down, red jets of flame spouted up among the houses which stood there, silent, without life. It was an eerie sight, no enemy guns, no movement in the streets, only the incessant rumbling of explosives. And then we went in. On both sides of the deserted streets, stood empty carcasses of burnt-out houses; glass, debris and tree branches were strewn on the pavements and in almost every street a building was burning like a huge torch.

'We arrived at a huge concrete surface shelter. These shelters are ugly, gloomy constructions with many floors above and below the ground where hundreds of civilians have been hiding for the last five weeks in darkness and stench. Army officers and the police had the entrance blocked and no one was allowed to leave the place. In the meantime the Gestapo and soldiers were looting the town, grabbing in mad lust the property of their own people, although there was no hope to carry it away. The Army refused to open the shelter. For several hours, it was besieged by American soldiers, then a German officer offered to surrender, if he was allowed to take away all his things, plus his batman.

'Lt Walker, a young company commander, made no effort to accept such a ridiculous offer and threatened to use flame-throwers. That helped. The doors opened and out came the drabbest, filthiest inhabitants of the underworld I have ever seen, as people came stumbling out into the light, dazed, then catching a breath of fresh air and finally starting to jabber, push, scream and curse. Some precipitated themselves on me, brandishing their fists. "Where have you been so long?" they shouted. "Why didn't you deliver us sooner from those devils?"

'It was a stunning sight. These were the people of the first German town occupied by the Allies. And they were weeping with hysterical joy among the smouldering ruins of their homes. "We have been praying everyday for you to come," said a woman with a pale, thin face. "You can't imagine what we have had to suffer from them." And then came the insults. "Bloodhound! Gangster! Bandit!" All this was the fruit of the beloved Führer. There is no one who can hate and curse so thoroughly as the Germans and these people were all green with hate of the Nazis. It was no trick. I certainly would not be cheated.

'It was the breakdown of a nation after having played for five years on the wrong cards. Maybe it was the rage of a gangster let down by his gangleader, but it was a hatred you only find in civil wars.'

But if the nameless Czech correspondent was confident that day that he was witnessing the 'breakdown of a nation', General Huebner, who was now faced with the final reduction of the city after the gap had been closed, was less than sanguine. Not only did he fear a major German counter-attack on the ring that had been thrown round the city, but the obstinate German resistance within Aachen to Seitz's probing attacks told him that his operations in the city itself would be no walkover. As he warned his staff officers, happy that evening of 16 October over their success at the gap: 'Total breakdown had not been achieved in Aachen yet.' Events were going to prove just how right the Commanding General of the 'Big Red One' was.

CHAPTER TWO

'OKAY, let's go, fellers,' the Lieutenant in German uniform whispered in pure American to the men behind him. Up ahead the night air-raid, which had been specially arranged to cover their penetration of the enemy line, was coming to an end.

He turned to the GIs of the 'Big Red One', who had smuggled him and his twenty-two men into the ruined waste of no-man's-land and then into the German line. 'Thanks, you guys. You can bug out now. We'll be okay.'

The GIs needed no urging. Somewhere or other, dug in in the shattered buildings, there were Rink's SS troopers and they knew what would happen to them if the SS boys caught them in the company of the Rangers dressed in German uniform. They whispered goodbye and slid back into the shadows, leaving Lieutenant Calagan, Sergeants Lasko and Bromfield, and the men to make out the best they could. One minute later, Lieutenant Calagan, or Schmidt as he was calling himself now, had done the same. The darkness had swallowed him and his men up and the daring operation had begun.

For several nights now, the headquarters of the OSS [the wartime forerunner of the CIA], located at nearby Heerlen, had been running little bands of Rangers, dressed in German uniforms, into Aachen to carry out special operations. Speaking perfect German, these Rangers had been trained in special schools just outside London where, among other things, they had learned how to carry out the sabotage ops which were to become their speciality in beleaguered Aachen. Now, at General Huebner's request, angered by the obstinate resistance offered by Colonel Wilck's men, the German-speaking Rangers had been destroying key German military installations within the city prior to the all-out attack on it by Huebner's infantry.

Equipped with German military identity discs, letters in German from their 'families' plus photos in their pockets, Lieutenant Calagan-Schmidt's Rangers had the task of destroying what was supposed by OSS Intelligence to be the main German signals centre, and a small elite German unit which was employed on this part of the front, whenever the American infantry broke through, as a special assault squad.

As the American air-raid came to an end, Calagan's Rangers edged their way ever closer to the centre of the city. But the going was difficult. Since they had been briefed for the operation at Heerlen two days before, American aerial and artillery bombardments had again changed the face of the city and they were forced to stop constantly and check their bearings in the shattered streets.

As they emerged from the immediate battle zone they were startled by a harsh voice demanding, 'Where are you going there?'

Calagan swung round, to be confronted by a large patrol of armed SS men, commanded by an *Obersturmführer*. The American Lieutenant caught himself in time. He clicked to attention and reported in the German fashion, '*Melde gehorsamst. Obersturmführer, erste Kompanie des ersten Bataillons!*' *

---

* 'Report respectfully, 1st Company, 1st Battalion.'

Above: He was lucky then: the book he was reading was pierced by a splinter of shrapnel, but Otto Pesch escaped unharmed. The photograph was taken in 1974.

Right: He was present at the last defensive position at 17 Weyhestrasse: Peter Schaaf.

Above: The last defensive position of the campaign leaders of Aachen: the bunker in Rutscher Street/Forster Street, as seen from Rutscher Street. *Below*: The entrance to the bunker seen close up. The building is today peppered with shrapnel. In certain places one can even make out the calibre of the half-burnt-out grenades.

General A. D. Gerhard Graf von Schwerin, former Commander of 116 Panzerdivision, photographed on November 17, 1974, in the parsonage at Vossenack-Eifel (Remembrance Sunday).

View from the Kapuzinergraben onto the Theaterplatz: 1944 (above), 1974.

The *Obersturmführer* waved him to relax. 'All right,' he snapped, 'Order your men to put down their weapons. And help over there. A bomb has collapsed the entrance to the air raid shelter. By the time the engineers get here, it'll be too late.'

'Jawohl Obersturmführer,' Calagan answered.

With a handful of German policemen and civilians they started to clear away the smoking debris. The police and civilians worked feverishly, expecting another enemy air raid at any moment. Calagan matched their frenzied energy, although he knew there would be no more American attacks that night. His men, on the other hand, felt nothing for the trapped German civilians. They set about the task carelessly and slowly, earning curses and threats from the Germans toiling in the debris and Calagan was glad when the entrance was finally cleared and he could withdraw his men.

Five minutes later he assembled them in a ruin and dressed them down, telling them that it was vital that they acted exactly like the ordinary German if they didn't want to find themselves propped up against a prison wall facing a firing squad.

By midnight they had destroyed the signals centre and were in position outside the building which they knew housed the elite German *Alarmeinheit.** Carefully they set up their two German Spandaus to cover the front of the building and waited for the signal. It came in the form of three red Very lights.

'Okay stand by,' Calagan whispered, as the flares started to fall to the earth. A moment passed. From the direction of the American lines, the artillery began to thunder, as if softening up the German positions prior to an infantry attack.

* Emergency unit.

The trick worked. There was sudden activity within the dark buildings opposite. Hurriedly the half-dressed Germans started to pour out into the night, struggling into their tunics, flinging their rifles over their shoulders, fumbling with their helmet straps.

Calagan's Rangers did not hesitate. At pointblank range they poured a murderous hail into the enemy. Germans fell everywhere, screaming in agony, caught completely off their guard. Still the machine guns hammered. It was murder.

Finally as the dying bodies piled ever higher in front of the entrance, Calagan yelled, 'All right, fellers, that's enough. Cease fire!'*

So, as General Huebner prepared his final offensive against Aachen, the nibbling process continued. On the morning of 17 October a group of engineers, stationed on the heights above the city, decided they would take a hand in the task of reducing Aachen's defences before the final assault. Two days before they had found an abandoned city tramcar in the city's Burtscheid suburb, bearing the line-number thirteen, and the idea of the 'V-13' had been born. For a day they had worked on it like enthusiastic schoolboys. On both sides they had painted its name 'V-13' in large letters. Next to it the tram now bore the words 'Berlin', plus an arrow pointing forward, and 'Aachen-Express'. In the doorway they had wedged a looted portrait of Hitler with the words 'Heil Heel' scrawled in black paint beneath it. But that wasn't all. The whole interior of the tram had been filled to the roof with captured German flak ammuni-

---

* Even thirty years later it is difficult to obtain information about Ranger Ops behind the German line at Aachen, possibly because during the Battle of the Bulge, the Germans used a similar trick. Any German posing as an American who was captured was shot.

tion, triggered to be set off by a time fuse once the V-13 hit its target.

That morning the engineers pushed their 'revenge weapon'* into position. As they visualized it, the V-13 would roll down the hill following the tramlines, take a right curve, gathering speed all the time, and crash right into the centre of Burtscheid. When they were ready the sergeant in charge set the time-pencil and gave the signal to start and they began to push the tram along the rusty tramlines. Slowly the ancient vehicle gathered speed. They watched it rattling down the height towards the German positions, careering wildly from side to side, as if it would jump from the rusty rails at any moment. Seconds later it whizzed round the curve and disappeared from sight. The engineers' eyes flew to the dials of their looted wrist-watches, as they timed the weapon's progress into Burtscheid.

Suddenly there was a tremendous explosion. The engineers ducked. The blast wave hit them in the face. Automatically they opened their mouths to prevent their eardrums from being burst by the pressure. Then they saw a brown mushroom of smoke rising into the air far short of the target. The V-13 had exploded prematurely! Despondently they set off to look for new homemade 'secret weapons'.

But all the weapons employed that day by the Americans in their 'nibbling away' process were not so ineffective. With his men still pinned down by the stiff German resistance at the Blücherplatz, Colonel Corley decided he, too, would employ a special weapon. It was a huge 155mm artillery gun.

Normally guns of that kind would be used far behind the front, from whence they could lob their monstrous shells a

* The name was taken, naturally, from the German *Vergeltungswaffen* (revenge weapons), V-1 and V-2 which were already beginning to fly over Aachen on their way to Liege and Antwerp.

distance of over five miles. Now Corley ordered the 1st's artillery to transport one right into the heart of Aachen itself. As one of the infantry fighting there at the time recalls: 'Resistance centred in the Technical High School* where fanatical Nazis were fighting from sewer to sewer. In the street-fighting it would take our big, self-propelled guns to clean them out. Nothing else would do the trick.' It did.

By noon that day resistance was beginning to crumble at the square as the gun pounded the German positions with frightening regularity. Down in the cellars of the Quellenhof, Colonel Wilck could feel the tremendous vibrations of the explosions, as shell after shell hit the German defences. Calling Koechling on the secret line, which the Rangers had failed to destroy because it was buried beneath the West Wall and known only to a few senior officers, Wilck told his Corps Commander that enemy self-propelled guns had surrounded his HQ on three sides and were firing at him at pointblank range.

Koechling reacted with alarm; he promised to send Wilck SS reinforcements and assault guns and told him to hang on as best he could. But reinforcements were not the Battle Commandant's primary concern that day. It was Corley's tremendous 155mm. It had shaken him considerably, although it was over half a mile away from the Quellenhof. But he didn't want to be trapped in the hotel when the Americans attacked. He wanted some excuse to move his HQ to the relative safety of the four-storey air-raid shelter made of reinforced concrete, located in the Forster-Rutscherstrasse, which he had already picked as his next HQ.

* He meant the *Technische Hochschule*, Aachen's celebrated Technical University.

That night the 'SS reinforcements' broke through to the Quellenhof, but they turned out to be men already under Wilck's command—Major Rink's 300 men of the 1st SS Battalion.

The SS men got off to a bad start. Assembling in the hotel's hot baths, where in peacetime rich men and women, suffering from rheumatic complaints, had enjoyed the heated springs which had once been used by the Romans, they found the building packed to the roof with supplies. SS man Peter Schaaf, born himself in Aachen, remembers today just how angry he and his comrades were at the sight. 'For days we had been fighting on meagre frontline rations while the gentlemen of the staff billeted in the Quellenhof had been feeding their faces in all sorts of delicacies.'

Swiftly the couple of elderly soldiers guarding the supplies were kicked about their business and the unshaven teenagers of the 'Adolf Hitler Bodyguard' began to loot the supply dump, Peter Schaaf filling his rucksack to the top with cigarettes and tobacco, ready for the battle to come.

Meanwhile Wilck and Major Rink met for the first time down in the cellar below the Hotel. It was not a happy meeting. Rink, stiff, and well aware that he belonged to an elite outfit, although Wilck outranked him, told the Colonel pointblank: 'I take my orders directly from the Head of the SS, Heinrich Himmler, *Oberst!* For that reason I can only place myself *conditionally* under your command.'

Wilck's face flushed. 'You are directly under my command, Major,' he retorted. 'I am Battle Commandant here and you are serving in this section of my front. How you combine that with any special orders you may have received from the *Reichsführer* SS is your problem.'

'I must protest,' Rink began. But before he could finish his protest, the alarm whistles began to sound and the two officers were forced to join the mixed defence team of People's Grenadiers and SS men to drive off a surprise American infantry attack, with both of them tossing grenades out of the Hotel's shattered upper floor windows like two ordinary 'stubble-hoppers'.

Thirty minutes later the alarm was over and the American patrol had been driven off, at the cost of only one casualty for the SS. Relative peace settled over the hotel once more. All the same Wilck felt very uneasy. Somehow or other he sensed that it was Rink's task to keep an eye on him. Not only would his family be in danger if he attempted to surrender now, but he too; for he was sure that Major Rink would not hesitate to put a bullet through his head if he even dared breathe the word *'Kapitulation'*.

CHAPTER THREE

Now as, unknown to each other, the Americans prepared their last attack on the city centre and General Koechling readied his desperate counter-attack, Field-Marshal von Rundstedt telephoned Koechling and told him to remind 'the Commander of the 246th Volksgrenadier Division once more and with the utmost emphasis that he will hold this venerable German city to the last man. *If necessary, he will allow himself to be buried in its ruins.*'

The warning was clear, but not only to Wilck. Koechling realized, too, that his own fate depended upon his successful relief of the besieged city. His counter-attack *had* to succeed!

In essence, he had planned a two-fold assault. From outside, the 3rd Panzer Grenadier and 116th Panzer Divisions would attack the American ring in the area of Verlautenheide and Ravelsberg. In the meantime the composite battle group made up of Rink's 1st SS and the survivors of the 246th Division's 404th Regiment, would counter-attack within Aachen itself. Jumping off from the area of the Passstrasse, the battle group would push into the northern end of the Farwick Park, close to the Quellenhof, and drive back the point of Colonel Seitz's 26th US Infantry Regiment, which was threatening to take the three key heights from which the Americans could dominate the whole city. It was a rough-and-ready plan, hastily thrown together and born of desperation. Yet both Koechling and von Rundstedt knew if it failed, Aachen would have to be abandoned to its fate.

That morning, Colonel Corley's riflemen moved into position in the Farwick Park area. Supported by the huge 4.2-inch mortars of a chemical mortar company, the men of the 'Big Red One' started to attack again. By midday they had captured the park's outbuildings, the greenhouses, now a mess of shattered glass, and the *Kurhaus*, where Peter Schaaf had found so much loot.

Now the infantry were in a position to launch a direct attack on the Quellenhof itself, still thought to be the German Main Battle HQ. But the Quellenhof, built thirty years before on the site of the Roman springs which had first attracted Caesar's legions to Aachen, was a tough nut to crack. The big mortar bombs simply bounced off its thick walls. In the end Colonel Corley, anxious to capture the hotel and move on to the key heights, ordered up one of the dreaded 155mms. Once it had carried out its deadly work, the infantry would outflank the shattered hotel and rush the hills beyond.

It was then that the teenage veterans of the *Waffen* SS hit the Americans dug in in the park. Supported by a couple of assault guns, they came forward boldly, as if nothing could stop them. Behind them Peter Schaaf, positioned at one of the Hotel's upper windows, fired belt after belt of machine-gun fire into the Americans, making them keep their heads down.

The Americans were caught completely off guard by the sudden attack. Their foxhole line was overrun. Wild cries, confused orders and counter-orders rose everywhere. An officer attempted to rally the men of the 'Big Red One'. Still the SS pressed home their attack. One of the German assault guns rumbled close to the American positions and started pounding them with its heavy gun.

The Americans began to break. Here and there the first scared riflemen clambered out of their holes and pelted towards the rear and safety. The SS pressed home their advantage, yelling triumphantly. The Americans gave in. An officer bellowed a frantic order to move back. The frightened infantry needed no second invitation. Covered by the grease guns of a few NCOs they pulled back across the Farwick Park in disorder. The young soldiers of the Adolf Hitler Bodyguard redoubled their efforts. The two assault guns rumbled to the front of the attack, with the infantry in their flying camouflaged capes tucked in tightly behind them in what the Germans called a 'grape'. Together they hurried forward, southwards.

They hit the next American company. Fighting raged around the American-held *Kurhaus,* built in the eighteenth century by Jakob Couven, an elegant structure which had seen the début of a young Austrian conductor named Herbert von Karajan, whom Hitler didn't like because he didn't 'use notes'.

The battle swayed back and forth. But in the end the Americans had to abandon it to the triumphant young SS men, who immediately started looking for American cigarettes and the much prized Hershey chocolate bars. Kicked out into the attack again by their NCOs, they pushed on against the Americans still holding the fringe of the park.

But not all the Americans had fled before their wild advance. A lone mortar observer of the forward American company refused to budge although the SS men were only a matter of yards away. Buried at the bottom of a foxhole, he whispered into his phone, giving the co-ordinates of his own position. With an obscene belch the 4.2 mortars opened up.

Great brown holes appeared suddenly in the park all around. Frantically the SS scattered, leaving behind some who were never to rise again.

More and more bombs rained down with deadly accuracy. Rink's officers tried to rally their men. Twice more they attacked, but the steam had gone out of their drive now. In the end they went to ground and began to dig in. Major Rink gave in. His men had thrown back the Americans and removed the threat to the Quellenhof for the time being. For the cost of a handful of dead and wounded, he had beaten them off and taken 35 prisoners from a formation, which he regarded as 'highly trained and experienced'.

Grateful for the respite, Colonel Corley reported to General Huebner personally that the German counter-attack from within Aachen had seemingly petered out. His men had held their own and he was confident that they would be able to resume their own attack by the morrow.

But by this time General Huebner was being faced by other and more pressing problems from outside. The alarming reports of a new German counter-attack along the Ver-lautenheide-Ravelsberg front were flooding in to his HQ. According to his forward companies, the Germans were not having too much success. All the same Huebner was worried. According to Divisional HQ Intelligence, these attacks might herald a major, all-out thrust to break through to the besieged city. Intelligence was also worried about the mysterious disappearance from the Aachen front of General Mueller's 9th Panzer Division, which had been there from the very start of the battle. Was it being prepared somewhere behind the line to aid the supposed German all-out attack?

Huebner put the fears of the Divisional Intelligence men to his Corps Commander. 'Lightning Joe' Collins, already

sick of the whole time-wasting Aachen operation and
worried by the ever-mounting casualties his other infantry
divisions were incurring in the green hell of the Hürtgen
Forest just below Aachen, decided to call off the final attack
for another forty-eight hours until he could bring reinforcements up to aid the Colonel's understrength regiment.
Ringing up General Maurice Rose, whose division was still
licking its wounds from the initial attack on the city, he ordered him to send two battalions of armour under the command of Lieutenant Colonel Hogan. Once the German
counter-attack from outside had been beaten back, Task
Force Hogan would lead the American attack on the domi-
nating Lousberg height.

A little later he called Huebner and told him to find additional infantry from somewhere or other along his long line.
Colonel Daniel's Battalion, which was already down to two-
thirds of its strength, would need 'additional muscle' if it
were going to be able to carry out its task of driving through
the centre of the city.

That night Colonel Wilck, too tired to worry even about
the threat to his life Rink seemed to pose, made a decision.
He had exactly 1,200 men left, including a hundred elderly
policemen. His armour consisted of one self-propelled gun,
and although his artillery spotters had been able to make
out two whole American batteries located in the ruins near
the Quellenhof, they couldn't knock them out; the defenders
had no ammunition left. Everywhere the cellars near the
Quellenhof were filled with dead and wounded and medical
supplies were running out rapidly. Thus it was that the 49-
year-old officer radioed his superiors: 'The situation in Aachen makes it probable that the last resistance will end on

1910 . . . Breakthrough via Soers will only be possible to-night . . . Request immediate decision. Wilck.'

Back at Koechling's HQ it was clear even to the thickest and most hidebound of his staff officers what Aachen's last Battle Commandant intended to do. If the counter-attack didn't succeed in breaking through, Colonel Gerhard Wilck would surrender once the Americans began attacking again!

CHAPTER FOUR

PEACE descended on the ruined city. The once magnificent oaks which had lined its avenues were gashed and broken. Great chunks of brickwork lay everywhere. The streets were littered with the debris of battle—the mutilated wrecks of tanks; burned-out trucks and half-tracks; and everywhere abandoned soldiers' equipment, German and American helmets, breadbags, K-ration cans, rifles, clothing; and the shapeless bundles in the gutter which had once been men. Now the only sound was the distant rumble of the artillery fire in the Hürtgen Forest and the occasional low boom as Rink's men destroyed the key railway bridges across the Kurbrunner, Burtscheider and Suedstrassen. Both sides were preparing for the final round. Aachen had exactly fifty-seven hours to live.

Amazingly life still thrived in the smoking ruins. In the egg-shape section of the city around the Quellenhof some three to four thousand soldiers and civilians were crammed together in the stinking cellars and bunkers.

Grenadier Peter Monschau, an 18-year-old soldier from nearby Düren, decided that morning to take advantage of the lull in the battle to search for food. Peter Monschau had arrived at the Aachen front on 27 September and had telephoned to his mother who had warned him: 'See if you can't get out of it. You might get hit and I've only got one son.' Since then he had tried to follow that maternal advice. In the first week he had wrapped his boots in rags because

some of his comrades had warned him that 'the *Amis* have
sensitive radio listening devices. They can even pick up individual soldiers by the noise their boots make.' He had also
avoided the deep bunkers like the plague, again on account
of rumours spread by his comrades, 'Don't go in there! At
night the *Amis*'ll come up with a gigantic bulldozer and
block the entrance with earth. Then you'll be really in the
mousetrap.'

Thus Peter Monschau had survived the real and imagi-
nary dangers of his first taste of battle. But now he was hungry. For the last two days he had been dug in in the Kurpark with nothing to eat but crackers and hard sausage, plus
a bottle of schnapps every second day. Yet once again he
was following the advice of his comrades who swore that
the Quellenhof was packed high with delicacies for the staff
officers who were living like 'God in France'; they even had
an inexhaustible supply of *Aachener Printen*. So with two
other comrades, the young Grenadier set off to look for food.

Cautiously they worked their way towards the hotel HQ,
the only sound the *Ami* loudspeakers on the other side of
the front, alternatively playing '*Lili Marlene*' and then ask-
ing them to surrender with the same old mixture of promise
and threat. 'Surrender! We guarantee fair treatment. You'll
be given good food and good quarters. If you don't, our Air
Force will bomb the Quellenhof and the Kurpark to bits.'
But at that particular moment Peter Monschau and his two
comrades were interested in neither the promise nor the
threat; their sole concern was the *Aachener Printen*.

The Quellenhof turned out to be a disappointment. The
staff officers weren't living like 'God in France'; they were
just as hungry as the frontline troops—and there was no sign
of the *Aachener Printen* anywhere. The three Grenadiers

were just about to leave the busy HQ when a staff officer stopped them.

'What are you doing here?' he demanded, taking in the filthy muddy uniforms and camouflaged helmets which indicated that they were frontline troops.

The three youths muttered something about having wanted 'to take cover' in the HQ. But the staff officer was not buying the lame excuse. He took their names and unit, and snapped: 'I think you were trying to dodge duty in the line. And you know what that means? All right, on your way, I shall be reporting this to your CO.' Sadly the three of them trailed back to their foxholes, knowing that if the officer reported them it could well mean the death sentence —'cowardice in action', they would call it at the court-martial.

But Peter Monschau was not destined to return to his unit. He and his pals had just reached the Park when they were surprised by an American patrol; and the way the Americans were gesturing with their machine pistols made it quite clear that they would not hesitate to use them. The three Grenadiers' hands shot into the air. They were soon searched and disarmed. Then the Americans started to herd them back towards their own lines. But Monschau was a little slower than his two comrades. Suddenly he felt a burning pain in his buttocks. He had gone too slowly for one of the Americans and had received the point of the man's bayonet in his right buttock to hurry him up.

Major Rink utilized the lull in the fighting to get most of his men out of the Quellenhof area. Wilck had already moved to his new bunker HQ and Rink was not going to sacrifice his precious SS troopers to defend an empty HQ.

Assembling the fifty unwounded survivors of his battalion, which had numbered 500 men two weeks before, he told them what he was going to do. They were going to leave the Quellenhof by the front entrance, crawl the length of the Ludwigsallee behind a small stone wall, which would hide them from the *Amis* until they came to the Bastei intersection. Here they would have to rush across the street in small groups and take their chance with the Americans who were keeping up an almost permanent hail of fire there. It was risky, but it was the only way out of the trap being laid at the Quellenhof.

Rink's men didn't hesitate. The Major was a tough, experienced soldier, who had got out of traps like this often enough before in Russia. If anyone could get them through, it was Rink.

That afternoon they set off for their new positions. They crawled the length of the Ludwigsallee behind the low ornamental wall without incident and assembled at the Bastei intersection. Just as Rink had predicted it was under permanent enemy fire. Somewhere in the ruins further up the street, the *Amis* had set up several machine guns, which hammered continually, sending a vicious stream of tracer at waist-height across the intersection.

The Major drew a deep breath. 'All right,' he commanded. 'You, you, you—you're coming across with me in the first group. If we get across safely, the rest of you will follow but at irregular intervals.' The men nodded.

'All right, here we go,' Rink snapped. '*Hals und Beinbruch!*'* Stooped double, the four SS men suddenly broke from cover. The *Amis* reacted just a fraction of a second too late. Before they could take proper aim, the men had flung

* Literally 'Neck and Leg Break', i.e. happy landings.

themselves full-length into the rubble on the other side of the intersection.

Rink rose to his feet, dusting the brick rubble from his camouflaged overalls, and waved his hand at the next group. They took a deep breath and belted across. Again they made it. Another group followed and another. Then it was the turn of the little group to which Peter Schaaf, a tall, young SS man who came from Aachen, belonged. He looked at his comrades' pale faces and knew they were thinking exactly the same as he was. Hadn't their luck run out by now? Wouldn't the *Ami* machine-gunners be waiting for them this time?

'All right,' the NCO in charge of the group ordered. '*Let's go!*'

Peter Schaaf sprang forward. The enemy tracer hissed towards them. Schaaf ran like he had never run before. The slugs struck up little blue sparks around his heels. To his right the NCO groaned and flung up his hands. He slammed to the cobbles. But nobody stopped to help him. Everyone was too concerned with saving his own neck. Schaaf rammed against the wall on the other side and hung there, his chest heaving wildly.

Half an hour later the 50 men of SS Battalion Rink were setting up their new HQ in the cellars of Number 17 Weyerstrasse on the steep southwestern slope of the Lousberg. With the rest of his comrades, Peter Schaaf toiled away to break through to the cellar of the next house, wondering whether he would survive what must come soon, little realizing that thirty years later he would be delivering heating oil to that same house in the course of his job as driver for an oil company.

That same afternoon, while Peter Schaaf dug into the cellar of the next house, preparing the defensive system that Rink had planned for his new HQ, another Aachener was forced out of his cellar at bayonet-point by a group of equally begrimed soldiers. The plump 53-year-old man had long been announced dead by the 'Greater German Radio'. But the man, who had always been an opponent of the Nazis in the fight between the Party and the Catholic church in Aachen, was not dead. In September he had refused to be evacuated by the SA; instead he had ordered his little band of loyal followers, who knew his cellar hiding place, to spread the rumour that he had been killed in the initial attack on the city he loved and had served so well. Now there was no need to hide any more. Although apparently a prisoner in a way he was free at last after eleven years of spiritual imprisonment.

As the six GIs of Colonel Corley's Battalion forced him out into the open in the Adalbertstrasse, he said quietly and without fear: 'I am the Bishop of Aachen.' The GI with the walkie-talkie contacted Corley's CP and asked what he should do 'with a bishop'. The answer was prompt and decisive. 'Treat him like a general.'

Bishop Johannes Joseph van der Velden smiled when he heard the words.

The news of the Bishop's capture was ordered to be kept secret by 1st Army HQ. (It was only revealed inadvertently by the BBC in the following January after the Bishop had celebrated high mass in Aachen's cathedral.) Thus the Allied correspondents, who had descended upon the city to report its fall, were reduced to reporting trivia. The correspondent of the *Daily Express* noted that 'a soldier with a wooden arm, and a captain, blind in one eye and unable to see well in the other, were captured today'. Reuters' correspondent (his own firm had been started in that same shattered city over a century and a half before), gave the details of his interview with a 25-year-old deserter, who told him: 'Four years of war are enough. We have had no water in Aachen for three days. The electricity is smashed too. We have been collecting rainwater or water from a pond. There is still food in many houses. Many of the leaflets [surrender leaflets] fired into the town yesterday drifted away, but the word went round quickly. The officers stopped us talking to the civilians and orders were given to fire on any civilian trying to leave the city. One NCO leaving with me was fired on by the SS. But we got away with one man wounded.'

Other correspondents reported that civilians told them that the young fanatics had fired on them because 'if we have to die, you can die too!'

It looked, if the correspondents were to be believed, that the final breakdown had arrived in the beleaguered city. Hitler's message to his people on 18 October indicated, too, just how serious the situation was on Germany's frontier. In his radio speech he declared: 'After five years of struggle, the enemy, helped by the defection of all our European allies, has at some points come near to Germany's frontiers and at others reached it.

'As in 1939, so now we stand alone to meet the blows of our enemy. At that time we succeeded by the first large-scale mobilization . . . Whereas the enemy believes that he can get ready for the last knock-out blow, we, on our part, are resolved to carry out a second large-scale mobilization of our people . . . We know the resolution of our Jewish international enemies to destroy us totally. We are meeting them with the total mobilization of all Germany . . . *I call upon all German men able to carry a weapon to make themselves ready to fight!*'

The German Home Guard, the *Volkssturm*, had been

born. Every male German between the ages of 16 and 60 had to report for duty with the new force, if he wasn't already in the armed forces. It was the last levee. Germany, it seemed, was on her knees.

General Clarence Huebner hoped so. Exactly twenty-seven years before, the 1st Division's artillery had fired the first shot of any American unit on a European battlefield. Now he wanted it to gain the honour of being the first to capture a major German city. On the same day that Hitler publicly announced the depths to which the *Wehrmacht* had descended, with his fresh infantry and Hogan's Task Force in position, he ordered Colonels Corley and Daniel to resume their assault on the morrow. Now the long and costly siege must come to an end speedily.

And in his new command post in the four-storey Rutscher-Forsterstrasse bunker, Colonel Wilck prepared his last order-of-the-day for the remaining 1,200 soldiers under his command.

It read: 'The defenders of Aachen will now prepare for the last battle. Forced back into the smallest possible space, we shall fight to the last man, the last grenade and the last bullet. In the face of the contemptible, despicable treason committed by certain individuals, I expect each and every defender of this venerable imperial city of Aachen to do his duty to the very end in fulfilment of our oath to the flag. I expect courage and determination. LONG LIVE THE FÜHRER AND OUR BELOVED FATHERLAND!'

CHAPTER FIVE

Dawn came with its usual October slowness. Crouching among the rubble, the waiting infantry of Colonel Seitz's 26th, wondered whether it was really growing light or whether their tired eyes were merely becoming accustomed to the darkness. But gradually the sky over the ruined horizon began to turn a dirty white. They began to stir, stretching bodies that were stiff and chill, wondering if it would be safe—there were still snipers about—to light the first cigarette of the new day.

The rain had stopped now. They pushed back their groundsheets and went to the nearest cover to urinate. Here and there men began to heat C-ration cans over flickering fires made from the cardboard containers in which the rations came. No one spoke. The infantry, who would lead the attack, were dirty and unshaven, totally unlike the Hollywood conception of the infantrymen. Everything was wet and cold and there was nowhere to sit down. Thus they stood around, their breath grey on the cold morning air.

To their front the ruins lay silent. There was no sign of movement in the brick waste which had once been a proud city. But the riflemen of the 'Big Red One' knew that somewhere out there in the rubble were men like themselves, wearing a different-coloured uniform but equally tired, worn and nervous, waiting for them to come so that the killing could begin for one last time.

A hundred and fifty yards away the defenders of the city

waited. Where it was safe to do so, the 'kitchen bulls' brought up hunks of hard, straw-filled army bread and containers of 'nigger sweat', as the German infantry called the bitter black ersatz coffee. Gratefully the defenders swallowed the hot brew.

Already the rumble of the first *Ami* guns heralded the start of the covering artillery barrage, which would sweep ahead of the enemy attack. Here and there the mortar bombs began to explode among the ruins. It wouldn't be long now.

'All right, you guys, let's move it!' Everywhere grumpy NCOs were moving among the American forward line, whispering the words the riflemen dreaded, 'Ten minutes to go.'

Slowly the first wave of Colonel Seitz's 26th Infantry formed up for the start of the attack.

At his advance CP in an Aachen suburb, General Clarence Huebner was already awake and alert. He knew the attack wasn't going to be easy, but this time he reckoned on success. The enemy had been compressed into a very narrow area, by now perhaps a mile square, with only one major axis for movement left to them, the Roermonderstrasse. Once his men attacked, Huebner reasoned that the German command structure would break down and the enemy leadership, which had been holding the defence together up to now, would be isolated. Soon the individual groups of German soldiers, cut off from their officers, would begin to surrender. Today General Huebner was confident that the 'Big Red One' would finally capture what was left of Aachen.

The Savelsbergs saw the first Americans come cautiously down the street in which they had been hiding these last five weeks. Wilhelm Savelsberg hastily put up the white flag which had almost caused his execution a month earlier. The advancing GIs grinned and waved to the two women. In their hands some of them bore looted flat irons, and they shouted in broken German, 'We want to make ourselves beautiful for the Frauleins!'

A German-American named James searched the Savelsberg house for 'Nazis'. When none were found there, he advised Wilhelm to copy out the words he scribbled down for him on a scrap of paper and put them on a large sign to be hung on the front door. Savelsberg followed his advice. Half an hour later the new sign hung on his front door. It read: 'There are no goddam Nazis in here!'

The Americans captured the ruined *Kurhaus* in a rush. They pushed on to the Quellenhof. While the paratroop defenders fled to the cellars to escape the direct American shelling by a 155mm at pointblank range, 2nd Lieutenant William Batchford rushed the lobby with his men.

The paras stumbled upstairs. Hand-to-hand fighting broke out in the entrance hall. Hand grenades flew back and forth. When the paras ran out of bombs, they started throwing empty champagne bottles from the cellars. But slowly they were pushed back, their dead littering the marble floor. Still they did not surrender.

Lieutenant Batchford called for machine guns. They were brought up and went into action at once, pouring a concentrated stream of fire into the basement where the surviving paras were still holding out. Now even they had had enough. With hands raised, their dirty, battleworn faces bitter with defeat, they began to come up, leaving 25 of their young comrades lying there dead.

Batchford's men ran up the great stairs, past the shattered furniture and broken windows, stamping over the glass debris in their combat boots. But apart from the dead crumpled everywhere in the upper floors, all resistance had ceased at the Quellenhof.

A GI pushed a dead gunner out of the seat of his quadruple flak cannon, which had been taken to pieces and reassembled upstairs, swung it round and started to pour a hail of 20mm shells into the German positions on the other side of the Farwick Park.

Below, the officers of the 'Big Red One', disappointed not to find Colonel Wilck in the Quellenhof, debated where exactly Aachen's Battle Commandant might be.

In his bunker, Wilck had just interviewed a wounded lieutenant and a sergeant, the sole survivors of their battalion. They had told him that the Americans were taking over farmhouses just beyond the Lousberg at the village of Soers. It was obvious what the enemy's intention was; he was going to try and rush the commanding height, from which he could dominate the whole of Aachen. Wilck turned to his radio operator. 'Send this message,' he ordered.

'Request immediate artillery fire on House Sonne, House Linde, House Scheuer and the Stockheide Mill.'

The radioman relayed his CO's instructions realizing how desperate the situation must be; for the first time Wilck was calling down fire on houses he knew were still occupied by his fellow Germans.

In one of those houses, Otto Pesch, a 27-year-old newspaperman recently released from the German Army on account of ill health after a long spell in Russia, was dividing his time between watching the slow advance of the *Ami* tanks towards Schloss Rahe—once inhabited by Czar Alexander I—and a novel entitled *Sheep in Wolf's Clothing*, when a sudden *Ami* dive-bombing attack drove him into the cellars. When he returned, he found the kitchen where he had been sitting covered in a mess of cottage cheese. An *Ami* shell had gone into a big container of the stuff and scattered it everywhere. Another smaller shell had penetrated the book he had just been reading, going through 120 of the book's 525 pages! Otto Pesch, destined to be Germany's first post-war newspaperman,* sat down, his face drained of colour.

Half a mile away, the first Sherman of the 3rd Division's Task Force Hogan swept into the courtyard of Schloss Rahe. It bore the brightly coloured flag of the 'Lone Star' State, which was not very surprising since it was the command vehicle of Lieutenant-Colonel Sam 'Bill' Hogan, a slow-talking Texan who looked a bit like a younger Will Rogers.

The shattered chateau was abandoned. But the signs of its former occupiers were everywhere. On all sides there were whisky bottles. But the expectant tankers' hopes were dashed abruptly. The bottles were all empty. The German defenders would be going to their death drunk. Hogan's Shermans rolled on to their objective—the Aachen–Laurensberg highway.

Down below, Wilck sent another message to his superiors: 'The battle group is defending itself stubbornly around the Lousberg, against an enemy who is attacking from all sides.'

'Stubbornly' was the right word. Now Wilck, accompanied by his batman Schulz, toured what was left of his front and saw with his own eyes just how tough a defence his men were putting up among the ruins. When he returned to his bunker that afternoon, having been forced to crawl back on his stomach, Schulz saw that his Chief had tears in his eyes.

---

* He was picked to edit the country's first newspaper to be licensed by the Occupation authorities, *die Aachener Nachrichten*.

Major Rink was no fool. He realized that Aachen had not long to live, and he was not going to spend the rest of the war in an Allied POW camp. That afternoon he decided he would start evacuating his wounded, a hindrance to any escape operation in the future. At his disposal he had seven half-tracks, which had been used to bring his men into Aachen at the beginning of the battle, now parked seventy yards from his Weyherstrasse HQ. He set a group of lightly wounded men to removing the mortars which were mounted on them and painting large red crosses on their sides.

While that was going on, he assembled the rest of his command in the cellar of his HQ. Swiftly he put them in the picture and then asked, 'Who can drive and knows Aachen? I need volunteers.'

Peter Schaaf did not hesitate. He could drive and he knew Aachen. 'I'll go, sir,' he said, raising his hand. That started the ball rolling. Eleven other young soldiers volunteered to attempt to break through the American lines with the wounded before it was too late, including Peter Schaaf's best friend, Willi Becker.

Rink nodded, 'All right, you move out at midnight. And as soon as you reach our own lines, report by radio. I want to know the route you took.' A plan was beginning to form in the Major's head. If the half-tracks containing the wounded could get through, then, when the time came, he could follow the same route with what was left of his command.

Midnight. Aachen was sinking in a sea of flames. Forty miles away in Belgian Hasselt, 14-year-old Rene Nikolai was awakened by his parents to come and look at the burning horizon and the searchlights sweeping the sky above Aachen like ghostly fingers. Thirty years later he still remembers the sight vividly.

To Peter Schaaf, helping to load his badly wounded comrades into the half-tracks, it seemed that the very bricks were glowing in dull-red with the intense heat. Finally they were ready and Rink gave them their last instructions. They were to take the same route out of the city as they had used to enter it. Once they ran into enemy opposition, they would have to make their own decision. He looked at Peter Schaaf and his mate Willi Becker in the lead half-track, laden with SS men who had lost their arms and legs. 'All right, Schaaf, off you go—and the best of luck.'

A moment later the half-track rattled off into the glowing darkness.

As he turned into the Roermonderstrasse, the only major road left in German hands, Schaaf put his foot down hard on the accelerator. Behind him the severely wounded men groaned as the cumbersome half-track began to gather speed. But Schaaf kept his foot pressed down on the floorboards. Soon they would be hitting the *Ami* lines and he wasn't going to chance his luck, in spite of the large red crosses painted clearly on both sides of the armoured vehicle. In front the north-western slope of Lousberg loomed up. Schaaf ducked instinctively. He knew that the *Amis* held most of the height now.

His caution was necessary. Suddenly an American machine gun opened up close by. Lead began to patter against the metal sides of the half-track. The wounded screamed in fear. Schaaf kept his foot down. Surely the *Amis* could see his red crosses by this light? Then, as abruptly as it had started, the machine-gun fire stopped. Schaaf breathed a sigh of relief. The convoy rattled on.

At the shattered café at the corner, Schaaf swung to the right. He would lead the convoy through the tunnel that ran under the railway line. There they would be protected from enemy fire for a few seconds at least. One by one the other half-tracks followed his lead. Suddenly three civilians leapt out of a trench dug into the entrance to the tunnel. 'What the devil are you doing here?' one of them screamed, recognizing the silver SS runes on Schaaf's collar. 'The *Amis* are everywhere!'

'Don't worry, old man,' Schaaf calmed him. 'We're in touch with them. We're taking out the wounded. 'Bye, we've got to get on.'

The convoy rolled through the tunnel, past pale, wide-eyed civilians who were sheltering there in scores. Now they were in the open again and beginning the climb up the height which led out of Aachen.

But then their luck ran out. A Sherman tank loomed out of the red gloom. Its crew spotted the German half-track at once. In an instant its electrically operated turret swung round. Its 75mm gun was trained on Schaaf's vehicle. In a second they would fire and blast him to extinction. Then the turret lid flipped open and a hand beckoned Schaaf to follow. The Sherman turned and began to roll up the hill, followed by the half-track convoy, passing tank after tank of Task Force Hogan, lined up carefully every four yards as if they were on parade. Schaaf looked at Becker. He nodded his understanding. They had not had a chance right from the start.*

At Wilck's HQ, Major Rink waited impatiently for news of the arrival of the convoy behind the German lines. None came. Towards dawn he asked Wilck, who kept the HQ's

---

* Two days later Peter Schaaf found himself in a special camp for SS men at Rheims. His American captors had allowed him to keep his rucksack filled with the precious stolen cigarettes and something else— a towel with the words HOTEL QUELLENHOF written on it in red letters. It is still in his possession to this day, his sole souvenir of the great battle for his hometown.

sole radio under his personal command, if he would check with 81st Corps HQ. Thirty minutes later the reply came through: 'Half-tracks with wounded cannot be found. Signed Roems, Chief-of-Staff'.

There was no way out of the dying city!

CHAPTER SIX

DAWN. Friday morning, 20th October, 1944. Slowly the Americans, creatures of habit who usually stopped fighting as soon as it grew dark and began again at first light, began their push forward towards Wilck's bunker, about which they had now learned from prisoners. Wilck and his surviving staff officers were keeping going on sheer nervous energy. As haggard, weary and dirty as their men, the officers started to hand out the daily ration of preludin tablets so that the defenders would be able to keep their eyes open. Some of them could not stand it any more. Alone in their waterlogged foxholes they succumbed to despair. Boot off, big toe crooked around the trigger of the rifle, its muzzle thrust in the mouth, a final pressure—and the misery was finally over.

Wilck tried to boost morale with decorations. That morning he requested fifteen Iron Crosses, first class, and 147 second class for his remaining eight hundred men defending the six hundred square yards around his bunker.

In their turn Koechling's staff officers tried to encourage Wilck. He was recommended by Koechling for the Knight's Cross of the Iron Cross and that morning the Corps' Chief-of-Staff radioed Wilck: '81st Corps expresses its greatest admiration for the brave defenders of Aachen, fighting to the last for Folk and Führer.'

Wearily Wilck replied: 'Thank you. Expect enemy attack

soon all along our tight front. The defenders of Aachen are prepared for the final battle. Wilck.'

Outside the stinking bunker, the flames had died down now. The morning was bright, clear and cold: a typical autumn morning in that part of the world. This day the Allied dive-bombers would be able to bomb the narrow circle of defenders around the bunker at will. But Corley and Daniel felt they could do without the dive-bombers now. While Corley's men pushed down the Weyherstrasse—finding Rink's HQ abandoned in the process—Daniel's infantry advanced towards the command bunker along the Rutscherstrasse. Soon they were in position to take the HQ under fire.

Corley had suffered casualties enough in the four-day battle for the city. He was not going to risk the lives of his worn infantrymen unnecessarily in a frontal assault on the bunker. Instead he ordered up one of his 155mm cannon. By midday it was in action, pumping shot after shot into the defences around the bunker at a range of less than two hundred yards. Soon it would turn its fire on the bunker itself. Slowly the 26th Infantry were ripping the guts out of the last defence of Aachen.

Night fell, a night of confused murder and mayhem. Cramped together in the top storey of the bunker, now overflowing with wounded, Colonel Wilck radioed a bold message, which was pitifully belied by the suffering all around him: 'All forces committed to the final struggle . . . The last defenders of Aachen, mindful of their beloved German homeland and with firm confidence in final victory, donate 10,468 Reichsmarks to the Winter-Help.* We shall fight on. Long live the Führer!'

---

* The Nazi relief fund to provide warm clothing for poor people. During the war it was used to do the same for the Army.

And on and on they fought that long night, as if their sacrifice meant anything in a world gone crazy and in which the victorious GIs outside were already using one hundred mark notes as latrine paper.

Another dawn. Saturday the 21st. Since the early hours Wilck had been carrying on a long conversation with the staff of his old division, the 246th People's Grenadier, located outside the city in safety. At dawn he advised them by radio: 'All ammo gone after severe house-to-house fighting. No water and no food. Enemy close to command post of the last defenders of the Imperial City. Radio prepared for destruction.'

The 246th replied: 'Long live the defenders of Aachen.'

Wilck sent his last message: 'We're reporting out. Best wishes to our comrades and our loved ones.'

The 246th just managed to get in its last message before Wilck ordered his radio operator to destroy the radio. It read: 'The 246th People's Grenadier Division expresses its gratitude and admiration for the effort and courage of its comrades. We salute you!'

Five minutes later the radio was destroyed and Aachen was finally cut off completely from the outside world. In the direction of Verlautenheide the German artillery had begun bombarding the American positions and Wilck knew that meant that the High Command had already given him up. But outside a strange silence had descended upon the battlefield. Even the great 155mm had ceased firing. It was the moment of decision.

While it was still dark, Rink had had his last talk with Wilck. Rink could see which way the wind was blowing in the bunker. On his return to his new CP in the Nizzaallee, he asked one of his remaining officers how much ammunition had they left. The lieutenant informed him that they could continue firing till about eight; then they would have nothing left.

Rink then gathered the handful of surviving SS men together and told them it was his first duty to save the Battalion. 'The Battalion'—all forty men of it—listened attentively as he explained that they would now break up into small groups and steal their way through the Allied lines in the area of Würselen in order 'to save this valuable human material for the Führer'.

Thirty minutes later the first group of this 'valuable human material' stole into the darkened street on the first leg of its long and adventurous journey. The SS was abandoning Aachen.*

Meanwhile Colonel Wilck was pondering an overwhelming decision of his own. He knew he no longer needed to fear Rink; he had read in the Major's eyes that morning that Rink had plans of his own. But what of his family if he surrendered? Would they be executed by the Gestapo? Now 80 years of age, ex-Colonel Wilck recalls: 'It was the most difficult decision of my whole life. But in the end I decided to surrender—and as a professional soldier, I had always regarded the act of surrender with the greatest of disgust.'

His decision made, Colonel Wilck was now faced with a new problem. *How?* Already two German officers, trying to surrender, had been shot down by the Americans although they bore a homemade white flag. Outside all was crazy confusion. In the end Wilck realized that the only way to do it was to ask for volunteers from the thirty-odd American prisoners in the bunker. Two men volunteered, both pris-

---

* Later Peter Schaaf was to hear in the special SS POW camp that Rink's men had finally broken through the American lines disguised as cowled monks, wearing habits they had looted somewhere or other in their trek out.

oners from the 'Big Red One', Sergeant Ewart Padgett and Pfc James Haswell.

A makeshift white flag was found for them. An English-speaking staff officer wished them good luck. The door to the bunker was opened cautiously. Taking a deep breath, the two GIs who had been in German hands for several days now, stepped outside. For a moment they blinked in the bright light.

Suddenly bullets started whizzing their way. Furiously they waved their white flag, and staggered down the debris-laden street towards the houses occupied by Corley's infantry. The firing stopped. Suspiciously a scruffy, unshaven rifleman leaned out of a shattered window nearby and waved them forward. Sergeant Padgett turned and beckoned to the German officer who was to accompany them. Minutes later they were behind the American lines relating their news to the first officer they could find.

Two hours later they returned and reported that the American command was ready to talk with Wilck. At approximately ten o'clock that bright autumn morning Colonel Wilck left the bunker alone. He was neatly shaven, his field grey uniform brushed and clean, contrasting strongly with the dusty, stained olive-drab of the American riflemen swarming all around him. Over his left shoulder he bore a camera.

A young American officer exchanged a few words in German with Wilck and led him to the only surviving house in Aachen's Hansemannsplatz, the house which was now Colonel Corley's CP.

With the aid of an interpreter Corley told Wilck that the Germans had treated their American prisoners in a very decent manner. He, Corley, would do the same and abide by the Geneva Convention. Thereupon he asked for Wilck's

pistol. But Sergeant Padgett had already beaten Corley to it.
With the American predilection for souvenirs, even at such
dramatic moments, he had nabbed the pistol outside the
house.

At that moment a jeep stopped outside with Wilck's batman, Schulz, an American driver, and the German Major
Heimann. Corley asked a final question: Had Wilck laid any
mines in the area of the bunker? Wilck replied in the nega-
tive and asked a question of his own. Could he speak to the
hundreds of German soldiers already being assembled outside ready for moving off to the POW cages? Corley said he
could.

Standing on the bonnet of the jeep which would take him
away, he explained his reasons for surrendering. In the end,
he told them, the defence of the ruined city was hopeless.
He wished them the best of luck for the future, then he allowed himself to be led to the jeep. A moment later he was
gone, heading for three years of captivity.

It was exactly five minutes after twelve on Saturday, 21st
October, 1944. The six-week battle for Aachen was over at
last. Across the border in nearby Belgium, the Belgian newspaper *La Nation* headlined the surrender with the words:
'*Aix-la-Chapelle n'existe plus!*'

CHAPTER SEVEN

ON that same afternoon, far away at the 'Wolf's Lair', Hitler's HQ buried in the forests of East Prussia, the Führer received the man who Allied Intelligence called the 'most dangerous man in Europe'. The year before, *Obersturm-bannführer* Otto Skorzeny had seized the Italian dictator Mussolini from his mountain-top prison. Now he had come to the 'Wolf's Lair' to report on his latest daring exploit: the kidnapping of Admiral Horthy's son and the seizure of the Budapest Citadel, the seat of the Hungarian government.

An enthusiastic Hitler, who had received the revised plan of the new operation he had named 'the Watch on the Rhine' that morning from his Chief-of-Staff Jodl, greeted him warmly. He looked at his huge visitor, his scarred face looking as if it had suffered at the hands of a butcher's apprentice gone crazy, and said: 'Well done, Skorzeny! I have promoted you and awarded you the German Cross in gold. Now tell me about Operation Mouse [the code-name of the Hungarian mission].'

Skorzeny described his kidnapping of the playboy Horthy's son in Budapest and how he had smuggled him out of his castle in a carpet. Hitler laughed a lot during his story, but when the scar-faced SS officer was finished and rose to take his leave, Hitler said, 'Don't go for a minute. I have perhaps the most important job of your life for you. So far very few people know of the preparations for a secret plan in which you have a great part to play. In December, Germany will start a great offensive, which may well decide her fate!'

Hitler explained his great new plan, the Watch on the Rhine, telling Skorzeny that the Western Allies now thought Germany virtually prostrate. But what if the 'corpse' should rise again and strike them such a crushing blow in the West that the British and Americans would be forced to sue for a favourable armistice? Hitler detailed the huge forces he had secretly built up while the Battle of Aachen had been going on. 'I'm telling you this,' he said, 'so that you realize that nothing has been forgotten. One of the most important tasks in this offensive will be entrusted to you. You will seize one or more of the bridges over the Meuse between Liège and Namur. To do so, you will have to wear British or American uniforms. The enemy has already done us a great deal of damage by the use of our uniforms in various commando operations. Only a few days ago I received a reliable report that the use of our uniforms by an American force had played no inconsiderable part in the attack on Aachen, the first German city in the west to fall into their hands.'

That afternoon, while the Minister of Propaganda, Dr Josef Goebbels, pondered gloomily how he should present the depressing news of the fall of Aachen to the German public (it took two days before he finally allowed it to be announced) *Obersturmbannführer* Skorzeny flew back to his own HQ happier than he had been for many a day. Thanks to the stubborn six-week defence of Aachen, Germany was going on to the offensive once again.

That day the final plan for the Battle of the Bulge was decided upon. The war, which Montgomery had wagered one week before would be over by Christmas, 1944, would last another seven months and before it was over, the United States Army would experience its 'European Pearl Harbor' in the snow-bound woods of the Ardennes, at the cost of 80,000 casualties.

AFTERMATH

CHAPTER EIGHT

It was what the Germans called *die Stunde Null*.* There was no transport, no gas, no electricity, no water, no post, no telephone. In the six-week battle nearly 80% of the remaining houses in Aachen had been destroyed or badly damaged. Commander Butcher, Eisenhower's public relations man, visited the city the week it surrendered and reported gleefully: 'The town is really beaten up to complete satisfaction. It has had numerous RAF raids by heavy bombers and our artillery and tactical air support had left fires still smouldering. As the frontline was still only 3,000 yards away, the town was subjected to periodic shelling and once we took shelter in a bombed-out building.

'We visited the headquarters of the Allied Military Government and found German men, women and children coming and going. They looked whipped. They were coming out of their cellars and gave evidence of really having "had it". We collected a few souvenirs for Christmas presents and departed for Maastricht.'

A more perceptive and sensitive visitor noted that same week: 'The city is as dead as a Roman ruin, but unlike a ruin it has none of the grace of gradual decay . . . Burst sewers, broken gas mains and dead animals have raised an almost overpowering smell in many parts of the city. The streets are paved with shattered glass; telephone, electric light and

* The Zero Hour.

trolley cables are dangling and netted together everywhere, and in many places wrecked cars, trucks, armored vehicles and guns littered the streets.'

While the victors closed a blind eye to the scores of Belgians and Dutchmen who had come over the border to plunder what was left of Aachen, taking away their stolen goods by the cartload, 1st Army Commander General Courtenay Hodges visited the famous Cathedral with his staff. To the surprise of the German guide, the General and all his staff bent their knees in front of the altar in the Charlemagne Chapel. Hitler had always maintained it was unworthy of a German to bend his knee before anyone.

Two months later the same Commander and his troops were taken by surprise by Hitler's December offensive. Sadly, the occupying soldiers vented their rage on the few civilians allowed to remain behind. Wilfully they set fire to empty houses and tossed furniture into the streets. With the German guns roaring just outside Aachen, the first modest attempts to rebuild the shattered city came to a rapid halt.

Still there were courageous men prepared to make another attempt. Lawyer Franz Oppenhoff was one. He allowed the Americans to make him the ruined city's chief burgomaster, although he confessed privately to his wife: 'The Nazis will already be briefing the paratroopers detailed to assassinate me.'

On Palm Sunday, March, 1945, his prediction came true. An SS commando of five men and one woman murdered him in his own house.*

But by that time, thanks to Oppenhoff, a new start had been made in Aachen. Already there were 20,000 civilians back in the ruins, a thriving black market and Germany's

---

* See the author's *Werewolf* for further details.

first free newspaper. The first modest attempts at rebuilding had begun.

In May of that year the war ended and Aachen became part of the British Zone of Occupation. The rebuilding process speeded up. New houses shot out of the ruins like mushrooms—more than forty thousand within a decade. Hotels, schools, new churches, to replace the 25 destroyed in the fighting, followed. The population increased rapidly—from 5,000 on 21 October, 1944 to the present 240,000.

Once more the ancient Imperial City started to attract important people, friends and ex-foes alike. Ageing Winston Churchill, who in March, 1945, had visited Aachen and nearby Jülich on his way to watch the great crossing of the Rhine, returned to accept the newly established *Karlspreis*, awarded annually to the statesman who had done most that year for European unity. In 1963, Edward Heath, who had once fought in the same area as the commander of an artillery unit, received the same prize for his efforts to take Britain into Europe.

Today Aachen is once again a great tourist attraction, flooded with visitors from all over the world in summer, snapping the sights with their cameras everywhere. But occasionally one can spot among the gay, careless throng, more serious elderly gentlemen in clearly transatlantic clothes bent over city maps, looking for other less obvious sights. They ask for places with names unknown to the modern Aachener, every second one of whom has been born since 1945—'Observation Height' and 'Crucifix Hill'.

For the war has been forgotten in Aachen. In the rebuilt Hotel Quellenhof, the guests know nothing of the young paras who fought their last battle against the men of the 'Big Red One', armed with empty champagne bottles, in the marble-floored lobby. Nor do the young, courting couples seated on the benches in the Farwick Park know—or care—about the even younger troopers of Rink's 1st SS Battalion who gave their lives so easily in that same place three decades or more before.

It is only when the informed visitor approaches Aachen University's 'Lab. for Machinery and Industrial Studies', located in the Rutscherstrasse, that the terrible past is reawakened. Next to the bell and the gate barring the entrance, there is a two-yard-broad hole in the thick concrete wall; within its centre a rusting steel projectile—the remains of one of Colonel Corley's 155mms. For the 'Lab. for Machinery and Industrial Studies', which is used by the University to carry out long-term tests of industrial equipment, is that bunker from which in another age Colonel Wilck surrendered the first German city into the Allied hands. It is all that is left of BLOODY AACHEN.

WHAT HAPPENED TO THEM?

COLONEL GERHARD WILCK, the last commandant of Aachen, is still alive. A hearty, lively 80-year-old today, his chief passion in life is his garden not far from the River Rhine. In 1976 his only office is that of chairman of the local gardeners' association.

His predecessor in command in Aachen is still alive too. After helping to create the new German post-war army, *die Bundeswehr*, Count Schwerin lives in Rottach-Eggern in Bavaria, a favourite place for pensioned-off German generals. But once a year he returns to Aachen to attend the reunion of the portly, white-haired men who once called themselves so proudly, 'The Greyhounds'—the 116th Panzer Division.

During that reunion the survivors always visit the nearby Vossenack Cemetery, where so many of their comrades are buried. There they pass grave number 1074, that of Field-Marshal Model, who had insisted so forcefully to Wilck that Aachen would be defended to the last and who recommended that Schwerin should be court-martialled.

Like all the other senior German commanders—Brandenberger, Schack, Koechling—he is long since dead, shot by his own hand in a lonely Westphalian wood, abandoned by everyone save his adjutant. 'After all, a German Field-Marshal does not surrender,' were his last words.

General Bradley, who that spring offered a decoration to

the soldier who brought in the fugitive Field-Marshal* is still with us, as are General Ernest Harmon, commander of the 'Hell on Wheels' and 'Lightning Joe' Collins, his West Point classmate, until recently chief executive of a large US corporation.

Some of the younger men are still to be found in the area of that city which played such an important rôle in their youth. Peter Schaaf, ex-member of the 'Adolf Hitler Bodyguard', drives his fuel-oil truck daily through that same chain of dragon's teeth, where Sergeant Dahl's Scorpion got stuck so long ago. Now many of them are painted a bright yellow and blue, the work of a young Dutch 'artist', whose aim it is to make its whole 285 kilometre length 'more friendly looking'. Occasionally Schaaf delivers oil to Rink's former HQ in the Weyherstrasse, pumping it into the same cellar where Rink once briefed him for his breakout attempt with the half-tracks.

Peter Monschau, the youthful innocent who had walked so blindly into the American trap after his unsuccessful search for the *Aachener Printen*, is now a police official in nearby Düren. Now and again he complains of a pain in his back where the impatient GI from the 1st Division had jabbed him with his bayonet that October afternoon.

He isn't the only one of the survivors who will bear the scars of that battle to his death. Ex-Pfc Robert Aldinger of the 'Big Red One', wounded in the head during the fighting, complained to his German friend Peter Marx on his last visit to the city in 1974 that he still gets persistent headaches in the temple where he was wounded.

Ex-Sgt Elmer McKay, who regularly visits his friend Josef Vohn, whose mother had offered him and his mates accom-

* After the surrender of the 'Ruhr Pocket' in April, 1945, Model went into hiding.

modation in her house after they had come out of the line
for a rest—'because she recognized in us equally scared,
motherless youngsters'—recalls how during that same rest:
'We played American football in a small field where one of
my friends broke his leg. Everybody congratulated him because now it was obvious that he had found an honourable
way out of continuing to be occupied in a very dangerous
business . . . as an infantryman! I can remember that nobody was interested in giving him any sympathy. We were
half jealous that we, too, were not lucky enough to break
our legs.'

But perhaps the most fitting memento to that battle is
that provided by Robert Cushman Jr. In the course of a tour
of Germany thirty years later, he went to look for the spot
on the River Wurm, where his father had been wounded
after receiving that telegram with the news that his wife
had given birth to a boy. Young Cushman found something
else as well—a German bride who returned home with him
to the states, perhaps the most convincing proof that the old
scars were healed at long last.

THE END